Writing Fun with Phonics

Encouraging Writing Using Phonics Skills

by
Dr. Jeri A. Carroll and Dr. Dennis J. Kear

illustrated by Becky Radtke

Cover by Becky Radtke

Copyright © 1992, Good Apple

ISBN No. 0-86653-686-8

Printing No. 98765432

Good Apple
1204 Buchanan St., Box 299
Carthage, IL 62321-0299

SIMON & SCHUSTER *A Paramount Communications Company*

Table of Contents

Why Teach Phonics? 1
How to Use *Writing Fun with Phonics* 3

Introduction to Beginning Sounds...4
Beginning Consonants 5
Activity Pages for Beginning Sounds....................................24

Digraphs and Blends 47
Beginning Digraphs 48
Blends..52

Word Families...57
Short Vowel Families 58
Long Vowel Families...71
Ending Blends 76
Other (ow/cow and oo/moon) 83

Writing Activities 85
Using Phonics Skills to Write *A* to *Z*, Digraphs and Themes...........86

Writing Center...142

Our families must be thanked for their patience and input. We appreciate the time they allowed us to spend away from home. In addition, the time we spent writing at home was carefully monitored by our young children who gave critical feedback. "What's that?" "You don't need that line there." "That must be for first graders." "I want to do that one."

GA1420

Why Teach Phonics?

One thing that years of research continues to tell us is that a knowledge of the alphabet (letters) and their sounds is strongly related to success in early reading. This is true regardless of the type of instruction used. If this is true, teachers of young children must teach phonics.

Does this mean that parents and teachers need only to teach children the alphabet and the sounds the letters make and success in learning to read is guaranteed? It would be wonderful if that were true, but unfortunately it is not.

Reading aloud to children appears to be the most important activity adults can do to help children develop the knowledge and skills they will need for learning to read. How often and what you read to your children also seems to make a difference. It is not just reading books to them that makes a difference, but enjoying the books with them and reflecting on their form and content. We need to model for children that we enjoy and value reading and that we hope they will too.

For children who enter beginning reading instruction with lots of prior experience with print, the letter-sound lessons in early reading instruction are little more than review of what they know rather than new information. The lessons are relatively easy and the purpose of the lessons is clear. The children's participation and motivation should be high.

Children who begin reading instruction with little knowledge about print are likely to have less interest in letter-sound lessons and less appreciation of these lessons. We can expect their learning to be slower and their attention to lessons shorter. For these children much of the content of these lessons will be new in detail and concept and, hence, more confusing and difficult to understand.

Children must learn that letters (the alphabet) represent sounds. This can be done by teaching the consonants in the initial position and in short words (two and three letters). Many consonants have a consistent sound (b, d, f, j, k, l, m, n, p, qu, r, t, v, z) especially in the initial position and in short words. Introducing the letters **y** and **w** as consonants will allow you to address the letter-sounds of twenty of the twenty-six letters in the initial position. **X** is very seldom seen in the initial position and certainly not in words that young readers often encounter. The alternate sounds of **y**, **w**, **c** (city), **g** (giant), **s** (sure), **h** (hour) can be delayed until the alphabetic principle, the knowledge that a symbol or letter represents one speech sound, has been established.

b d f j k l m n p qu r t v z

GA1420

The vowels are irregular in the English writing system. However, when the vowels occur singly in three-letter words, they most often take on a regular, "short" sound. Most phonics-emphasis programs teach the short vowels early in the instructional program. The long vowels in this book are presented in association with word families.

Word families allow young children to read sets of new words by changing only the first sound, a sound that they are familiar with. Once they recognize the family from which the word is derived, the process is simple.

Silent letters (w, gh, k) should be taught by giving students practice with relevant words.

Writing

Encouraging students in independent writing is a worthwhile activity that will help develop necessary skills for both reading and writing. Because printing is such a slow process, children often voice the sound or name of each letter as they print it. This voicing of the sound or name of the letter while it is being printed helps bind the visual, motor and phonological images of the letter together.

Children who are encouraged to use invented spelling and independent writing become more aware of the sounds of letters and eventually better independent writers than those children who are forced to write each word correctly spelled. Writing and invented spelling exercises may significantly improve children's attitudinal and language readiness for reading.

Both copying and tracing letters are of some value but help letter recognition less than independent writing. This is because copying and tracing can be done without thinking about the letter's sound, name and shape. Children should be encouraged to get whatever they can on paper to represent what they are saying or thinking.

GA1420

How to Use *Writing Fun with Phonics*

What makes this book different?
Most beginning phonics books encourage the recording of isolated sounds. Activities in this book encourage the child to use invented spellings (how he thinks the word might be spelled) using whatever knowledge of phonics he knows. Writing is stage-like in young children. The order is as follows: scribbling, letter-like symbols, simple use of some phonics, more sophisticated phonics and then "adult" spellings.

Parents are reminded that their children are using their own knowledge of phonics at the bottom of each page where children are being encouraged to use invented spellings.

This book is divided into four sections—beginning consonants, blends and digraphs, word families and writing activities.

The first section utilizes beginning consonants.
First, children are asked to identify a picture that begins with a particular sound, circle the picture and write the word by phonetically sounding it out, helping children link the letter and its sound. Teachers are given names of pictures in a word box that may or may not be copied for the children.

For other activities children are asked to think of a word that begins with a letter, draw the picture of the word and write the word by phonetically sounding it out. Children must use their phonics skills to sound out these words before they can draw pictures.

For some activities children are asked to generate a list of words or pictures beginning with a particular sound or to write a story whose topic begins with a certain letter.

The second section introduces digraphs and blends.
Students are asked to identify a picture that begins with a sound or think of a word that begins with the sound, circle the picture and write the word by phonetically sounding it out.

The third section contains word families.
Children are asked to put a beginning consonant in front of the family to form a new word and to illustrate the word. Children must use invented spellings as they phonetically spell words.

With long vowel families, ending blends and other vowel teams, children are asked to do four things: (1) write the word family after the beginning sound, (2) write the beginning sound in front of the word family, (3) write the word by sounding it out and (4) phonetically sound out the word to illustrate it.

The last section contains activities that encourage children's writing.
These activities are set up so that the teacher can cut them out, mount them and display them in a writing center or use them as extension activities throughout the day.

For center activities utilizing phonics skills
Learn and Grow from A to Z, a companion to this book by Kathy Dunlavy, Good Apple, 1992.

GA1420

Introduction to Beginning Sounds

A very important goal of phonics instruction is for children to acquire the understanding that a letter represents a sound. Since it is difficult to explain this to young children, it is necessary to practice it in a variety of ways. This concept can best be illustrated through the study of consonants and the sounds they represent. In the initial position and in short words (two and three letters). single consonants have basically one sound for each letter. We have included the regular consonants and **y** and **w** in the initial position.

The letter **x** is introduced in the final position because there are very few words where it is in the initial position. This allows us to address the twenty-one of the twenty-six letters through activities in this section.

At least one activity in the section addresses each vowel in the initial position, allowing the children or the teacher to choose short, long or both as the assignment.

Many of the following pages have a word box containing the focus words. You may want to cover this box and delete it from the page to make the exercise more challenging for your children.

In this section children are asked to identify a picture that begins with a particular sound or think of one themselves, circle the picture and write the word by phonetically sounding it out. This helps children link the letter and its sound.

For some activities children are asked to generate a list of words or pictures beginning with a particular sound or to write a story whose topic begins with a certain letter.

Here's an example.

4

GA1420

Bb

Circle the pictures that start with **b**.
Using the Word List, write the word in each box below.
If you have time, draw more **b** pictures on the back
and write the word for each.

Word List

bat	bed
bib	bug
box	

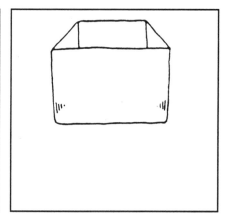

B -----------------------------------

b -----------------------------------

Note: Your child may have used his/her knowledge of phonics to spell some of
these words like they sound.

Cc

Circle the pictures that start with **c**.
Using the Word List, write the word in each box below.
If you have time, draw more **c** pictures on the back
and write the word for each.

Word List

cat   cup
candy   cut

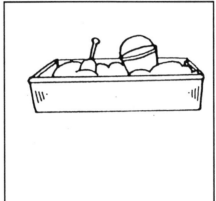

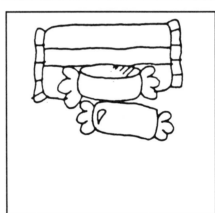

C –

c –

Note: Your child may have used his/her knowledge of phonics to spell some of
these words like they sound.

Dd

Circle the pictures that start with **d**.
Using the Word List, write the word in each box below.
If you have time, draw more **d** pictures on the back
and write the word for each.

Name _____

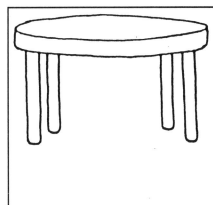

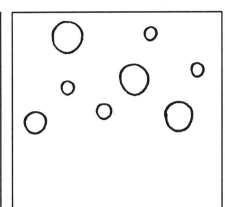

D _____

d _____

Note: Your child may have used his/her knowledge of phonics to spell some of
these words like they sound.

Draw a word that begins with **f** in each box below.
Use the words in the Word List if you need help.
Write the word in each box below.
Cut out the big **F**.
Glue it on a piece of construction paper.

Cut out the big F!

Name _____

F _____

f _____

Note: Your child may have used his/her knowledge of phonics to spell some of these words like they sound.

GA1420

G g

Name _____

Circle the pictures that start with **g**.
Using the Word List, write the word in each box below.
If you have time, draw more **g** pictures on the back
and write the word for each.

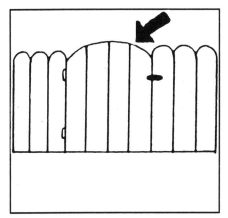

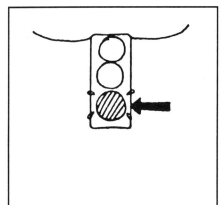

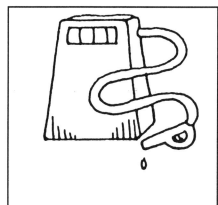

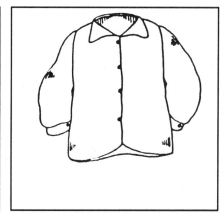

G -

g -

Note: Your child may have used his/her knowledge of phonics to spell some of
these words like they sound.

Draw a word that begins with **h** in each box below.
Use the words in the Word List if you need help.
Write the word in each box below.
Cut out the big **H**.
Glue it on a piece of construction paper.
Use scrap paper to practice writing Hh.

Word List
hub	hog
hunt	hand
hill	hat
hit	hen

Note: Your child may have used his/her knowledge of phonics to spell some of these words like they sound.

Jj

Circle the pictures that start with **j**.
Using the Word List, write the word in each box below.
Color the pictures.
If you have time, find some **j** words in your reader and write them on the back.

Word List	
jet	jam
jacks	jog

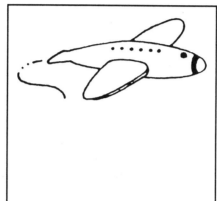

J _____

j _____

Note: Your child may have used his/her knowledge of phonics to spell some of these words like they sound.

Kk

Circle the pictures that start with **k**.
Using the Word List, write the word in each box below.
If you have time, draw some pictures on the back that start with the **k** sound and write the word for each.
Some might start with **c**.
If you have time, color the pictures.

Word List	
kick	kid
king	kilt
kiss	

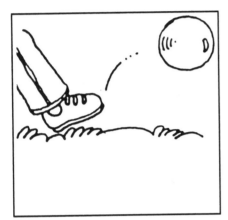  

K _____

k _____

Note: Your child may have used his/her knowledge of phonics to spell some of these words like they sound.

GA1420

Draw a word that begins with **l** in each box below.
Use the words in the Word List if you need help.
Write the word in each box below.
Cut out the big **L**.
Glue it on a piece of construction paper.

Word List

lamp	lock
land	lodge
lap	lollipop
leg	lunch
lip	lookout

Name _____

L _____

l _____

Note: Your child may have used his/her knowledge of phonics to spell some of these words like they sound.

GA1420

Mm

Read the words in the box below.

Circle the words you know.

Using the Word List, write one word in each of the boxes on this page.

Draw a picture of each word.

Word List	
map	mutt
mop	men
mask	mitt
milk	mug
man	mud
mist	malt

Make more **m** pictures on the back. Label each picture.

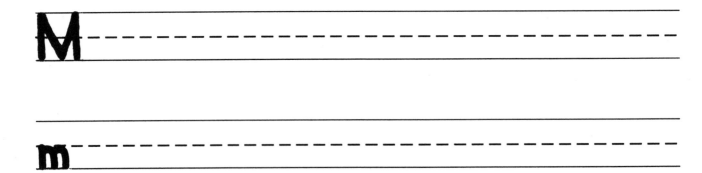

Note: Your child may have used his/her knowledge of phonics to spell some of these words like they sound.

Nn

Read the words in
the box below.

Circle the words you
know.

Using the Word List,
write one word in
each of the boxes
on this page.

Draw a picture of
each word.

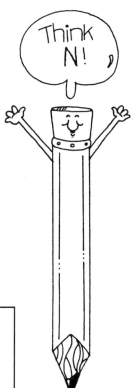

Word List

nap	nice
nut	nickel
nod	north
nab	neck
nasty	napkin
necklace	

If you know any more words, write
them on the back and draw pictures
for them, too.

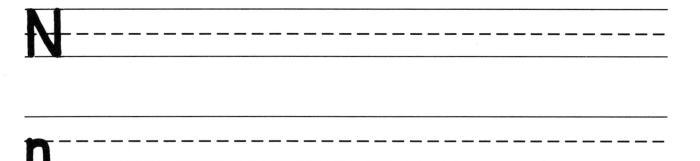

Note: Your child may have used his/her knowledge of phonics to spell some of
these words like they sound.

P p

Read the words in the box below.

Circle the words you know.

Using the Word List, write one word in each of the boxes on this page.

Draw a picture of each word.

Let's draw p pictures!

Word List

pig	pansy
pills	pans
picnic	pat
pack	pets
pot	putt
potato	pick

Make more **p** pictures on the back. Label each picture.

P _____

p _____

Note: Your child may have used his/her knowledge of phonics to spell some of these words like they sound.

Qq

Name _____

Circle the pictures that start with **qu**.
Using the Word List, write the word in each box below.
If you have time, cut out some **qu** words and glue them on the back.

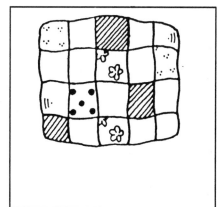

Q _____

 _____

Note: Your child may have used his/her knowledge of phonics to spell some of these words like they sound.

GA1420

Rr

Using the Word List, write the word in each box below.
Color the pictures of the words that start with **r**.
Think of other **r** words. Write them on the back and
draw pictures of them.

Word List

rip   red
rock   rug

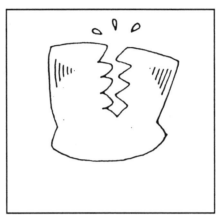

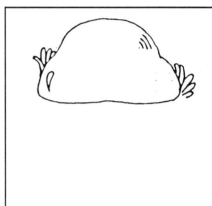

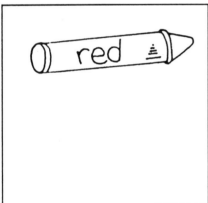

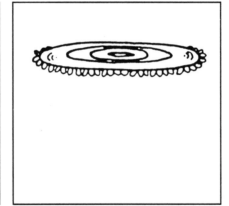

R _____

r _____

Note: Your child may have used his/her knowledge of phonics to spell some of
these words like they sound.

GA1420

S s

Circle the pictures that start with **s**.
Using the Word List, write the word in each box below.
If you have time, draw more **s** pictures on the back
and write the word for each.

Word List

sack	sun
six	sunk
sign	

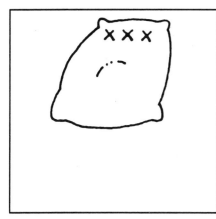
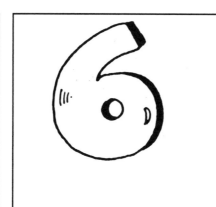

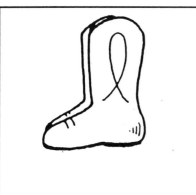

S -

s -

Note: Your child may have used his/her knowledge of phonics to spell some of
these words like they sound.

Copyright © 1992, Good Apple

19

GA1420

Draw a word that begins with **t** in each box below.
Use the words in the Word List if you need help.
Write the word in each box below.
Cut out the big **T**.
Glue it on a piece of construction paper.

Word List

track	top
tag	twin
tacks	trunk
ten	tusk
tent	truck
tickle	treetop

Cut out the big T!

Name _____

T _____

t _____

Note: Your child may have used his/her knowledge of phonics to spell some of these words like they sound.

GA1420

Circle the words you know in the Word List.
Write one word in each box below.
Draw a picture of each word.

VYZ

Word List	
van	yes
vest	yell
vet	zip
yam	zebra

Vv _____

Yy _____

Zz _____

Note: Your child may have used his/her knowledge of phonics to spell some of these words like they sound.

GA1420

Xx

Circle the pictures that end with **x**.
Using the Word List, write the word in each box below.
Color the pictures that have an **x** in them.

Word List	
ax	box
mix	six

 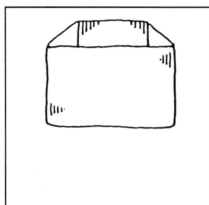 

  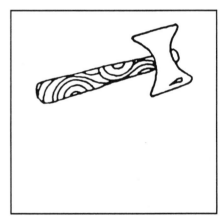

X —

x —

Note: Your child may have used his/her knowledge of phonics to spell some of these words like they sound.

W w

Circle the pictures that start with **w**.
Using the Word List, write the word in each box below.
If you have time, cut out some **w** pictures and glue
them on the back.
Write a word for each.

Word List	
wax	web
wet	win
watch	

W _____

w _____

Note: Your child may have used his/her knowledge of phonics to spell some of
these words like they sound.

Aa

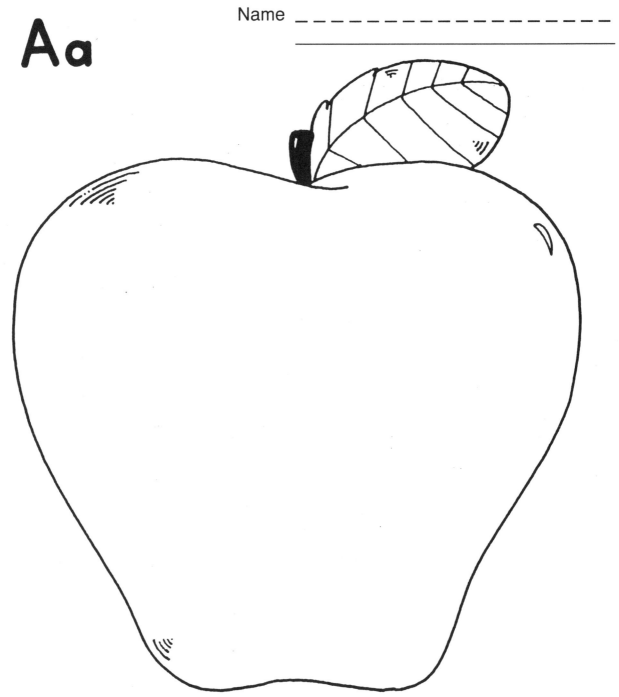

Choose one.
1. Write as many **a** words on the apple as you can.
2. Draw as many **a** words on the apple as you can.
3. Glue as many **a** words on the apple as you can find.
4. Write a story about apples using as many **a** words as you can.
When you are finished, cut out the apple and put it on your bulletin board.

Note: Your child may have used his/her knowledge of phonics to spell some of these words like they sound.

24

GA1420

Bb

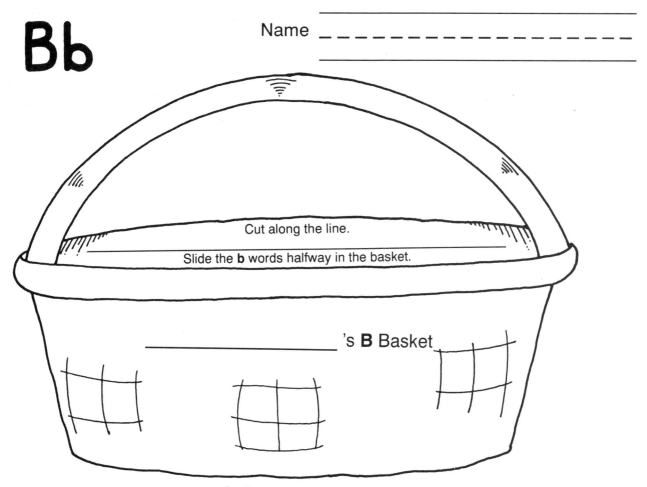

Cut along the line.

Slide the **b** words halfway in the basket.

_____ 's **B** Basket

Color the pictures that begin with **b**.
Write the words at the top of each box. Cut off the bottom of this page.
Cut out the **b** boxes. Put them into the basket.

Note: Your child may have used his/her knowledge of phonics to spell some of these words like they sound.

Cc

C Caterpillar

Write a **c** word in each circle.
Draw a picture of each word.
Cut out all the circles and the head.
Glue the parts together to make a **c** caterpillar.

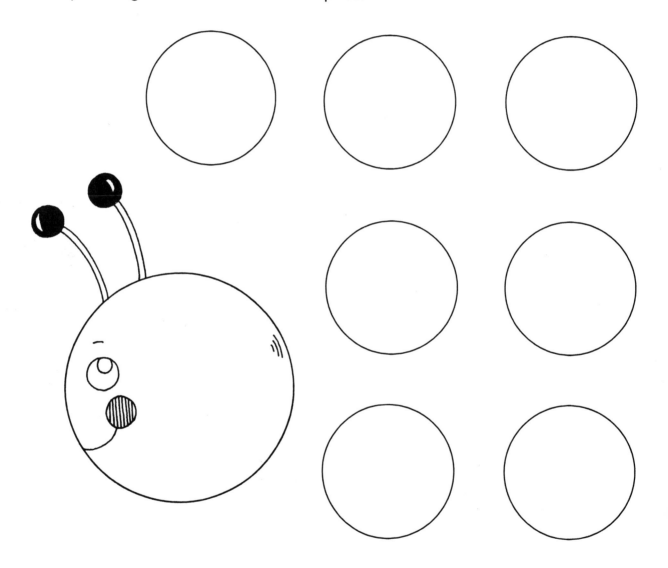

Note: Your child may have used his/her knowledge of phonics to spell some of these words like they sound.

GA142

Dd

Decorate the door with "d" words.

Find **d** words.
Color them.
Cut them out.
Glue them on the door.
Write the word for the picture under the picture.

_____ 's Door

Note: Your child may have used his/her knowledge of phonics to spell some of these words like they sound.

GA1420

Ee
Ee

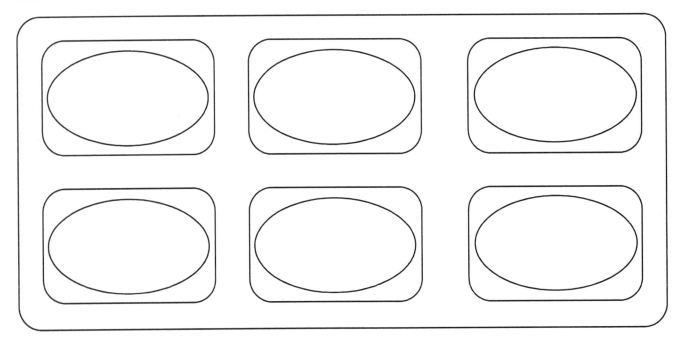

Look at the eggs below. Write the words for the **e** pictures. Cut out the **e** eggs and glue them in the carton above.

Note: Your child may have used his/her knowledge of phonics to spell some of these words like they sound.

GA142

Ff

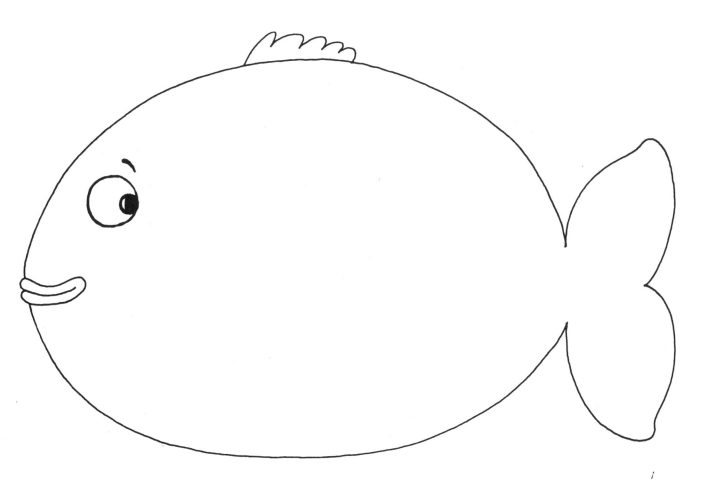

Choose one.
1. Write as many **f** words on the fish as you can.
2. Draw as many **f** words on the fish as you can.
3. Glue as many **f** words on the fish as you can find.
4. Write a story about fish using as many **f** words as you can.
When you are finished, cut out the fish and put it on your bulletin board.

Note: Your child may have used his/her knowledge of phonics to spell some of these words like they sound.

Gg

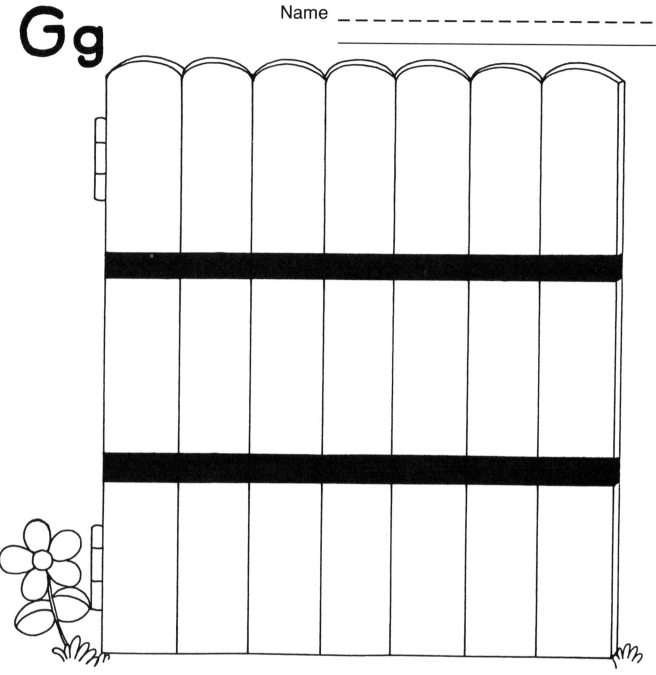

Choose one.
1. Write as many **g** words on the gate as you can.
2. Draw as many **g** words on the gate as you can.
3. Glue as many **g** words on the gate as you can find.
4. Write a story about what's behind the gate using as many **g** words as you can. When you are finished, cut out the gate and glue it onto a sheet of paper. Draw the rest of the picture for your story.

Note: Your child may have used his/her knowledge of phonics to spell some of these words like they sound.

GA1420

Color all the pictures that start with **h**.
Write each word by the picture.
Trace the path from dot to dot of the **h** pictures to see what you get.

Note: Your child may have used his/her knowledge of phonics to spell some of these words like they sound.

31

GA1420

Ii

Choose one.

1. Write as many **i** words on the igloo as you can.
2. Draw as many **i** words on the igloo as you can.
3. Glue as many **i** words on the igloo as you can find.
4. Write a story about living in an igloo. Use as many **i** words as you can.

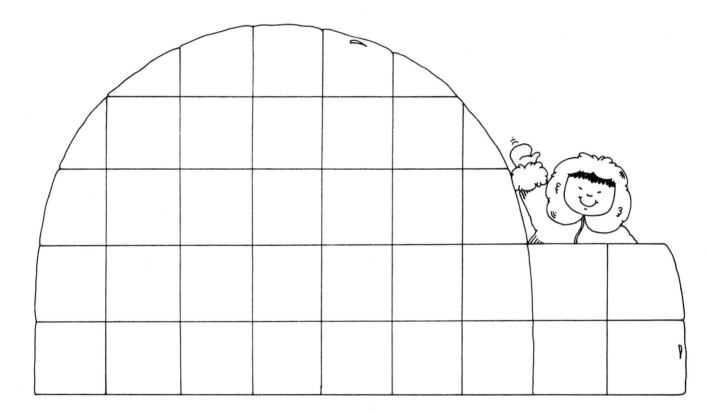

Note: Your child may have used his/her knowledge of phonics to spell some of these words like they sound.

Jj

J Jar

Write a **j** word on each jelly bean.
Draw a picture of each word on the jelly bean.
Draw more jelly beans in the jar if you know more words.
Color the jelly beans your favorite flavors.

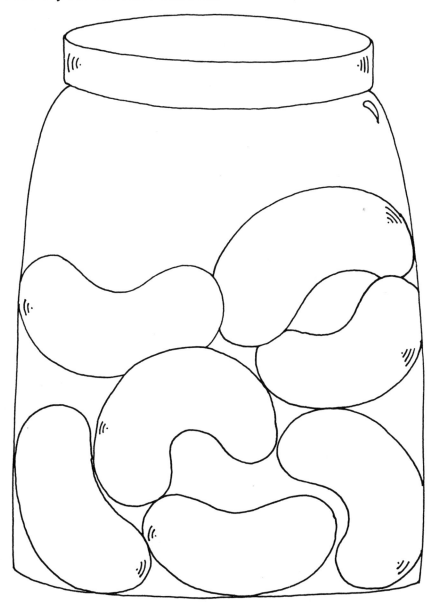

Note: Your child may have used his/her knowledge of phonics to spell some of these words like they sound.

33

GA1420

Kk

Name _____

Write a "k" word on each kite.

Write more **k** words here.
If you have time, draw a
picture for each word.

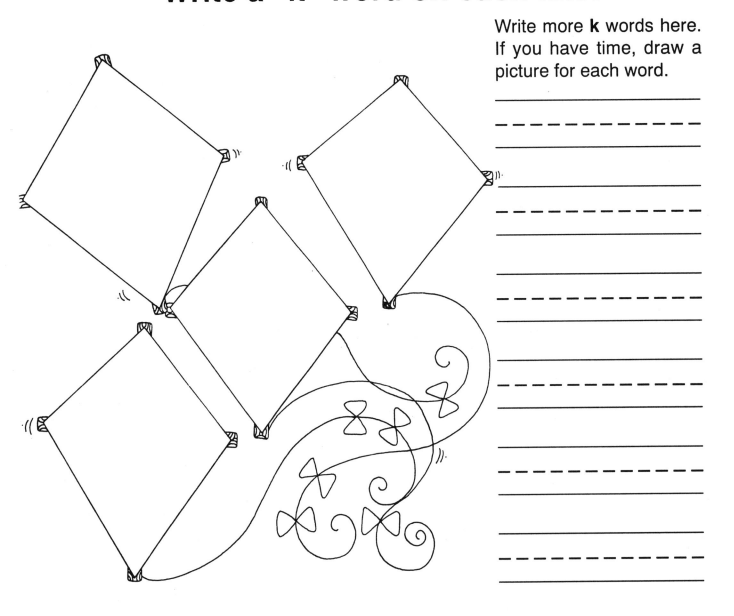

Note: Your child may have used his/her knowledge of phonics to spell some of these words like they sound.

34

GA1420

LI

LI

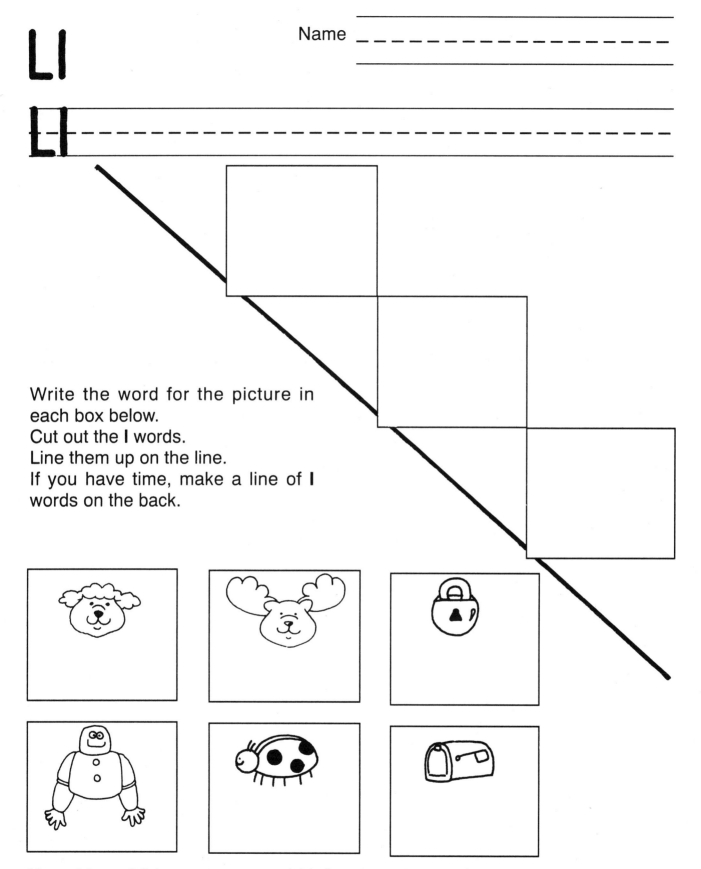

Write the word for the picture in
each box below.
Cut out the **I** words.
Line them up on the line.
If you have time, make a line of **I**
words on the back.

Note: Your child may have used his/her knowledge of phonics to spell some of
these words like they sound.

35

GA1420

Mm

Help the mouse move through the maze to its mom.

Circle all the words that start with **m**.
Write the words on the lines beneath the pictures.
Trace the path from the mouse to its mom.

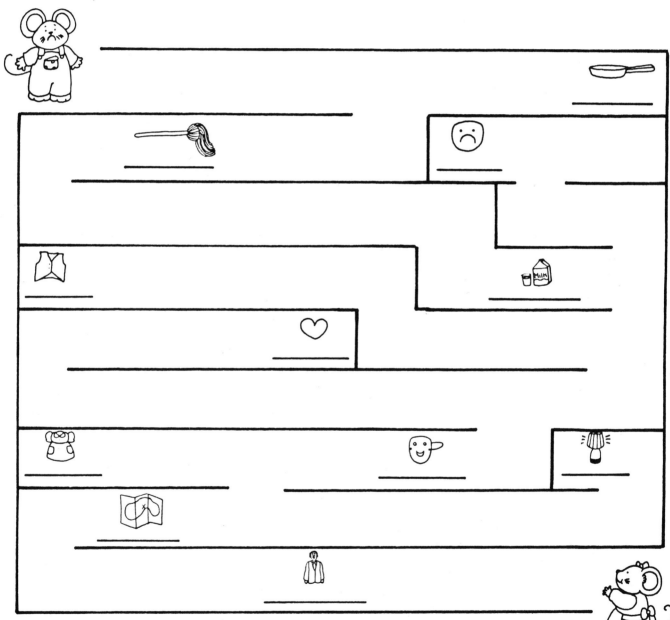

Note: Your child may have used his/her knowledge of phonics to spell some of these words like they sound.

Nn

News

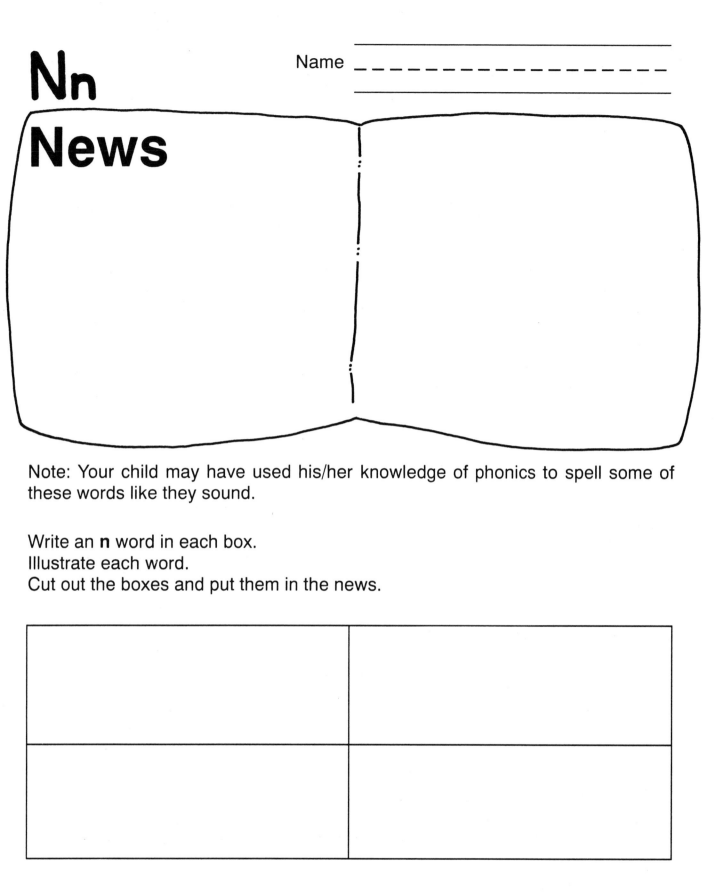

Note: Your child may have used his/her knowledge of phonics to spell some of these words like they sound.

Write an **n** word in each box.
Illustrate each word.
Cut out the boxes and put them in the news.

After you cut off this bottom part, turn your paper over and put more **n** words on the back page of your news.

GA1420

Oo

Name _____

Choose one.

1. Draw an **o** picture in each box and write the word.
2. Write a word with a short **o** in the middle in each box and illustrate each word.
3. Write a word with a long **o** in the middle in each box and illustrate each word.

Note: Your child may have used his/her knowledge of phonics to spell some of these words like they sound.

GA1420

Pp

Help the pig down the path to its pen.

Circle all the words that start with **p**.
Write the words on the lines beneath the pictures.
Trace the path from the pig to its pen.

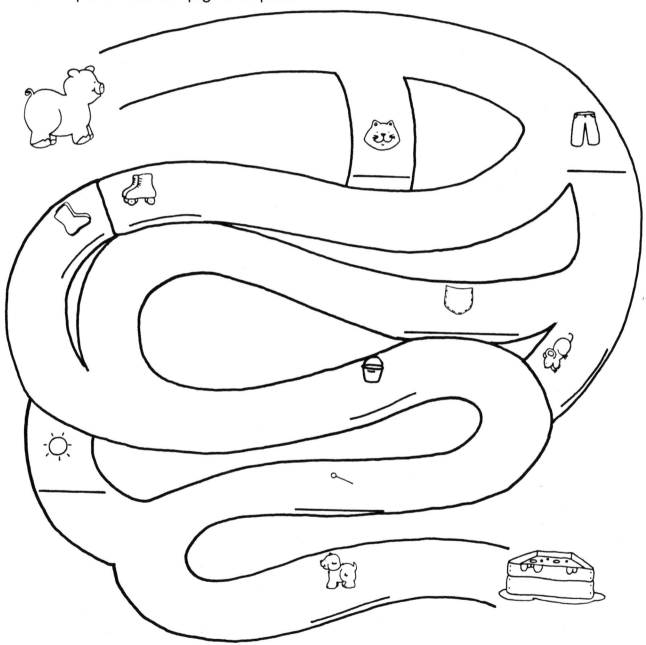

Note: Your child may have used his/her knowledge of phonics to spell some of these words like they sound.

Qq

Q Quilt

Write a **q** word in each quilt square.
Draw a picture of each word in the square.
Cut out all the squares.
Glue the squares onto 4" x 4" (10.16 x 10.16 cm) wallpaper squares.
Glue them all onto a 9" x 12" (22.86 x 30.48 cm) piece of construction paper.

Note: Your child may have used his/her knowledge of phonics to spell some of these words like they sound.

Rr

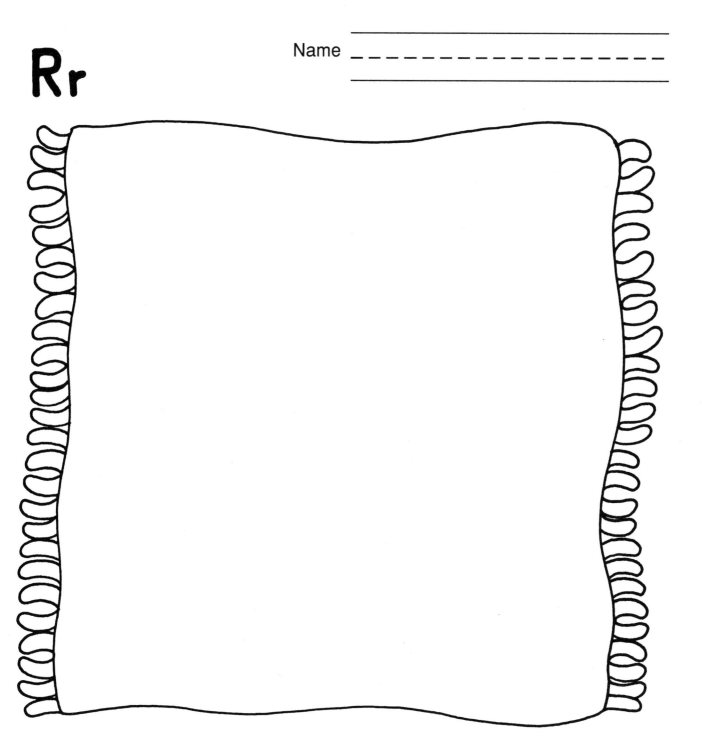

Choose one.

1. Write **r** words all over the rug.
2. Draw **r** pictures all over the rug. Write the word for each.
3. Cut out **r** pictures from a magazine. Glue them on the rug. Write the words.
4. Write your favorite story on the story rug.

Note: Your child may have used his/her knowledge of phonics to spell some of these words like they sound.

GA1420

Ss

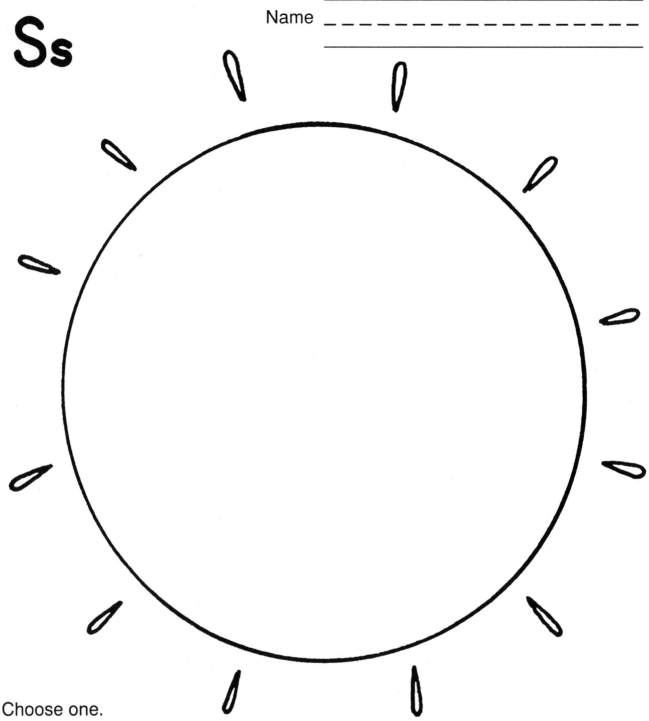

Choose one.

1. Write **s** words all over the sun.
2. Draw **s** pictures all over the sun. Write the word for each.
3. Cut out **s** pictures from a magazine. Glue them on the sun. Write the words.
4. Write a sunny day story on the sun. Use as many **s** words as you can. Underline them.

Note: Your child may have used his/her knowledge of phonics to spell some of these words like they sound.

GA142

T t

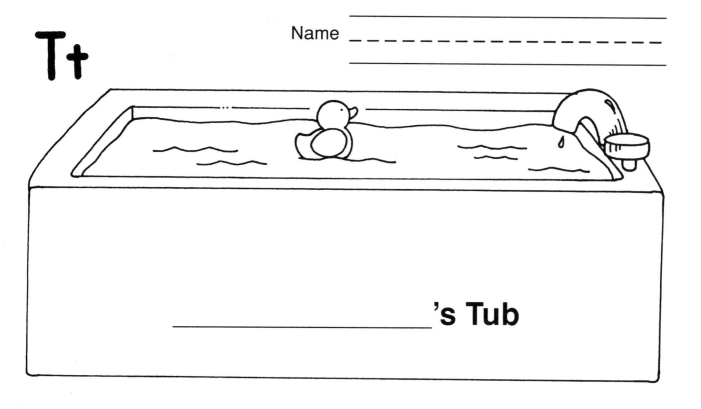

_____'s Tub

Color the pictures below that begin with **t**.
Write the word at the top of each box.
Cut them out.
Cut out the tub above.
Glue the words on the back of the tub.
If you have more space, draw some more pictures and write their words.

Note: Your child may have used his/her knowledge of phonics to spell some of these words like they sound.

GA1420

Uu

Think of as many **u** words as you can.
Write or draw one on each raindrop.
Cut them out and glue under the umbrella.

**Under
the
Umbrella**

Note: Your child may have used his/her knowledge of phonics to spell some of these words like they sound.

44

GA142

Vv

Choose one.
1. Write **v** words all over the van.
2. Draw **v** words on this van. Write the word for each picture.
3. Cut out pictures that start with **v** from magazines. Glue them on the van.
4. Write a moving van story. Use as many **v** words as you can. Underline them.

Note: Your child may have used his/her knowledge of phonics to spell some of these words like they sound.

 **W w**

Name _____

Color the watermelon green.
Cut it out.
Color the back red with black seeds.

Choose one.
1. Etch **w** words all over your watermelon after you have colored it green.
2. Cut out pictures that start with **w** from magazines. Glue them on the watermelon.
3. Write directions for eating a watermelon on a 4" x 6" (10.16 x 15.24 cm) sheet of paper. Glue it on the watermelon.

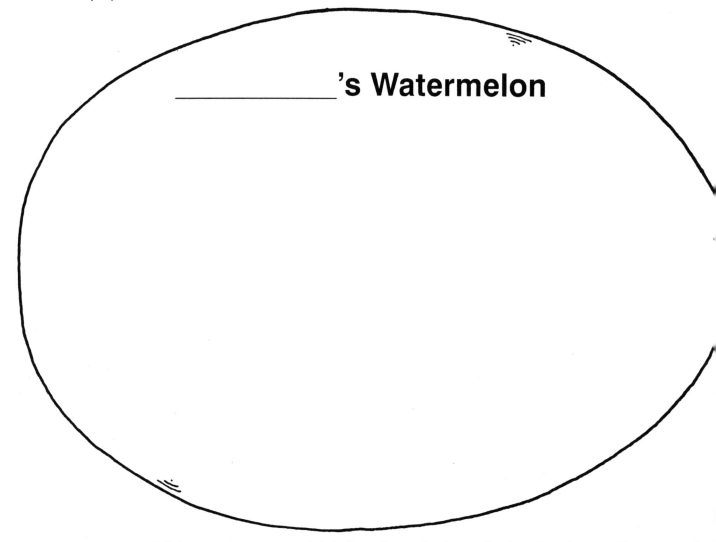

_____'s Watermelon

Note: Your child may have used his/her knowledge of phonics to spell some of these words like they sound.

Copyright © 1992, Good Apple

46

GA142

Digraphs and Blends

Two consonant letters that represent one sound are called consonant digraphs. The digraphs **ch**, **sh**, **wh** and voiceless **th** (as in thin) are included in this section. The voiced **th** (as in this) is not included because there are few short words containing this sound in the initial position. Also, none of those few words can be pictured easily.

Consonant blends or clusters are two or more consonant letters that represent a blended sound. Each of the letters in the cluster is sounded in the order it appears within the word (glass). **L** (blue), **r** (grass) and **s** (sport) blends are included in this section.

The consonant digraphs and clusters included in these lessons are common sounds contained in a number of primary reading programs. Students are once asked to identify a picture that begins with a particular sound or think of a word themselves that begins with the sound and write the word by phonetically sounding it out.

Here's an example from the "sh" page.

shirt

GA1420

ch

Name _____

Circle the pictures that start with **ch**.
Using the Word List, write the word in each box below.
Color the pictures.
If you have time, find some **ch** words in the dictionary
and write them on the back.

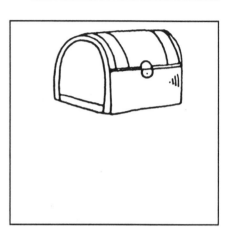

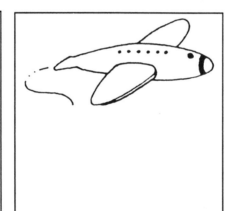

Ch -----------------------------------

ch -----------------------------------

Note: Your child may have used his/her knowledge of phonics to spell some of
these words like they sound.

GA142

sh

Name _____

Circle the pictures that start with **sh**.
Using the Word List, write the word in each box below.
If you have time, cut out some **sh** words and glue
them on the back.

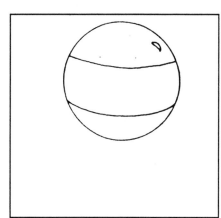
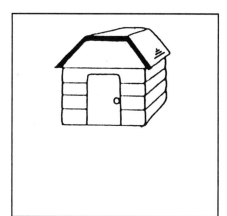

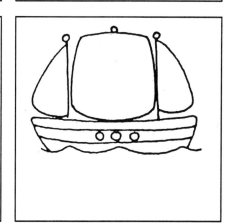

Sh _____

sh _____

Note: Your child may have used his/her knowledge of phonics to spell some of
these words like they sound.

th

Name _____

Circle the pictures that start with **th**.
Using the Word List, write the word in each box below.
If you have time, write some **th** words on the back.
Draw a picture for each word.

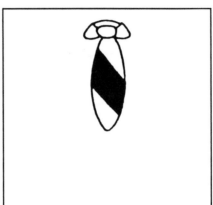

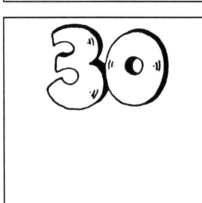
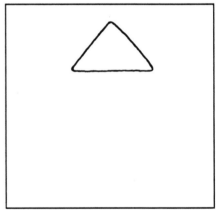

 Th _____

th _____

Note: Your child may have used his/her knowledge of phonics to spell some of these words like they sound.

wh

Circle the pictures that start with **wh**.
Using the Word List, write the word in each box below.
If you have time, draw a whale on the back.
Cover it with **wh** words.

Word List	
whip	white
whale	whistle
whisker	

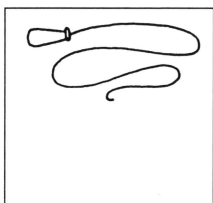
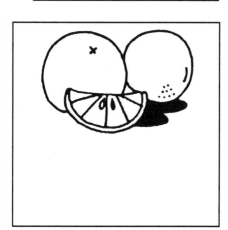

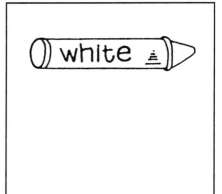

Wh _____

wh _____

Note: Your child may have used his/her knowledge of phonics to spell some of these words like they sound.

GA1420

Name _____

"L" Blends

Draw a picture in each box that starts with one of the blends below. Write the word in the box.

bl _ _ _ _ _ _ _ _ _ _ _ _ _ _ _

gl _ _ _ _ _ _ _ _ _ _ _ _ _ _ _

cl _ _ _ _ _ _ _ _ _ _ _ _ _ _ _

pl _ _ _ _ _ _ _ _ _ _ _ _ _ _ _

sl _ _ _ _ _ _ _ _ _ _ _ _ _ _ _

fl _ _ _ _ _ _ _ _ _ _ _ _ _ _ _

I'm a capital "L"... and I'm a lowercase "L"!

GA1420

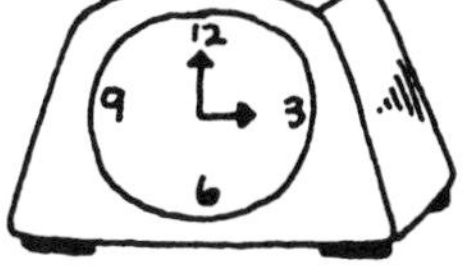

Name _____

cl _____

cr _____

Look at each picture.
Write the word in the box.
Color the pictures.

Can you think of more words that start with **cl** or **cr**?

Write them in this space.

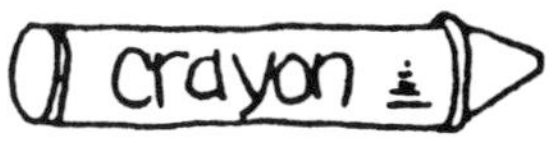

crayon

cream

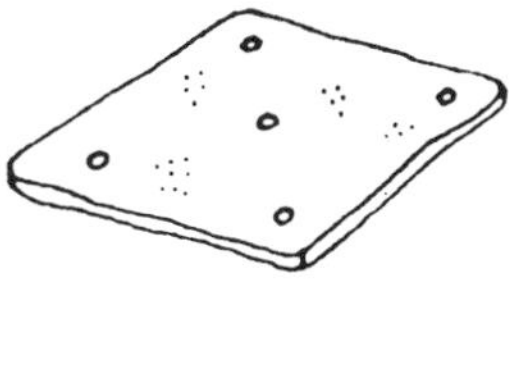

Closed

GA1420

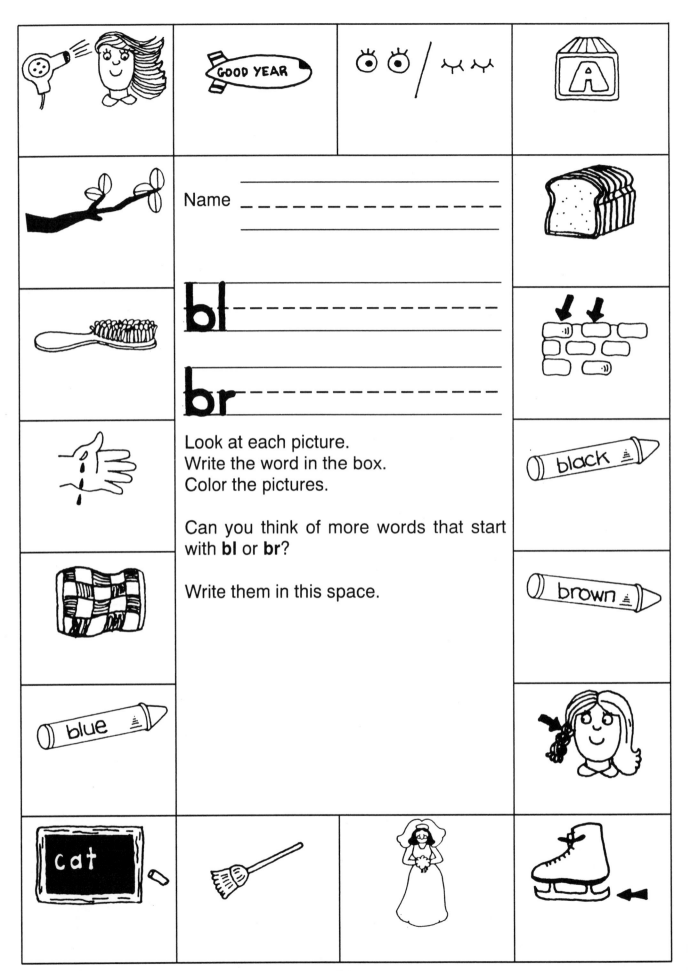

Name _____

bl ------------------------

br ------------------------

Look at each picture.
Write the word in the box.
Color the pictures.

Can you think of more words that start
with **bl** or **br**?

Write them in this space.

black

brown

blue

cat

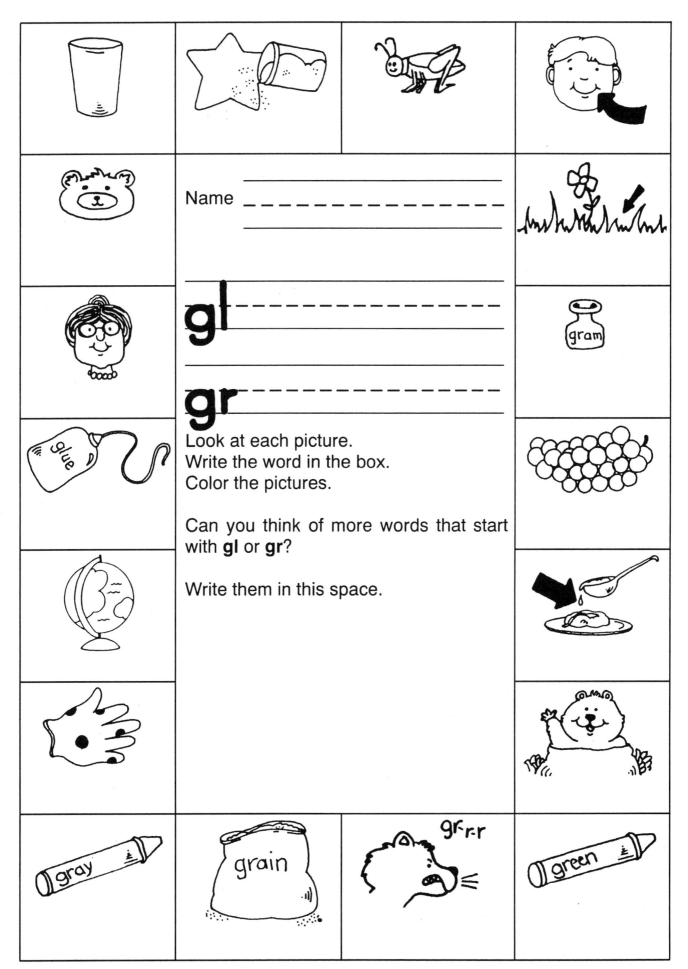

Name _____

gl - - - - - - - - - - - - - - -

gr - - - - - - - - - - - - - - -

Look at each picture.
Write the word in the box.
Color the pictures.

Can you think of more words that start with **gl** or **gr**?

Write them in this space.

gram

glue

grain

gray

green

gr r-r

55

GA1420

Name _____

sl _____

sp _____

Look at each picture.
Write the word in the box.
Color the pictures.

Can you think of more words that start with **sl** or **sp**?

Write them in this space.

Slam

slate

GA1420

Word Families

Children generally find it easy to learn to read words using word families, or phonograms. The vast majority of the phonograms found in primary texts contain vowel sounds that are consistently pronounced the same way in every word in which they appear. These consistent phonograms are contained in well over a thousand words found in the speaking vocabularies of primary grade children. Approximately five hundred primary grade words can be derived from a set of only thirty-seven phonograms.

In these activities children are asked to put a beginning consonant in front of the family to form a new word and then asked to illustrate the word. In this way, once again children will be using invented spellings as they phonetically spell the words.

When dealing with long vowel families, ending blends and other vowel teams, children are asked to do four things: (1) write the word family after the beginning sound, (2) write the beginning sound in front of the word family, (3) write the entire word by sounding it out and (4) phonetically sound out the word to illustrate it.

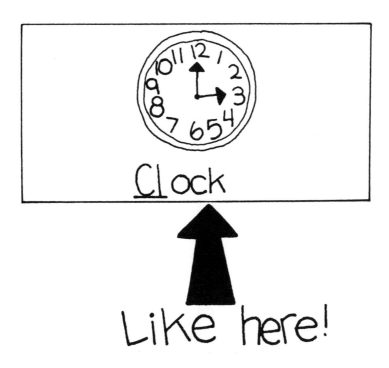

57

GA1420

-ab

Write each of the letters below in front of ___ **ab** in each box. Draw a picture of each word.

c   d   j   l   t   gr   sc   sl

__ab	__ab
__ab	__ab
__ab	__ab
__ab	__ab

If you have time, on the back change the ___ **ab** to ___ **at** and make some new words.

ab ➡ at

GA1420

-ock

Name _____

Write each of the letters in front of ___ **ock** in each box. Draw a picture of each word. Cut out the word boxes. Glue them in alphabetical order on a strip of paper.

bl cl cr d kn l r s

__ock	__ock
__ock	__ock
__ock	__ock
__ock	__ock

Block is an **ock** word. Draw a picture on a sheet of paper of something you can build with blocks. Label your picture. Try building the picture you made with blocks.

Copyright © 1992, Good Apple

59

GA1420

-ed

Write each of the letters below in front of ___ **ed** in each box. Draw a picture of each word.

b   f   l   r   sl   w

__ed	__ed	__ed
__ed	__ed	__ed

Cut these words off.
Glue them on the back.
Draw a picture of each.
Connect the picture and the word with a line.

shed   sled   sped   fled   bled

GA142

-uff

Write each of the letters below in front of ___ **uff** in each box. Draw a picture of each word.

b bl c fl gr h

__uff	__uff	__uff
__uff	__uff	__uff

When you add a **y** to the word *fluff* you get *fluffy*.
On the back draw pictures of six fluffy things.

61

GA1420

-ug

Write each of the letters below in front of ___ **ug** in each box. Draw a picture of each word.

b d h j m r

_ug	_ug	_ug
_ug	_ug	_ug

Bug is an **ug** word.
Draw six different kinds of bugs on the back.
Label each one.

GA142

-ill

Write each of the letters below in front of ___ **ill** in each box. Draw a picture of each word.

b   d   f   h   w

_ill	_ill	_ill
_ill	_ill	_ill

If you have time, paste one of these words in each corner on the back.
Draw a picture of each word on the page.
Connect the picture with the word.

shrill   skill   spill   still

63

GA1420

-ell

Write each of the letters below in front of ___ **ell** in each box. Draw a picture of each word.

b f s t w y

_ell	_ell	_ell
_ell	_ell	_ell

Sometimes people make wishes in wishing wells.
Make a list of wishes you would make on the back.

-um

Write each of the letters below in front of ___ **um** in each box. Draw a picture of each word.

b g h r dr pl

__um	__um	__um
__um	__um	__um

Gum is a fun **um** word.
Draw six different kinds of gum on the back.
Label each one.

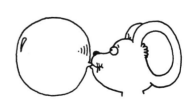

GA1420

-in

Write each of the letters in front of ___ **in** in each box. Draw a picture of each word.

b ch gr p th t w

___in	___in
___in	___in
___in	___in
___in	___in

Cut out the boxes below. Glue them on the back. Draw a picture.

 in a box   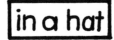 in a hat   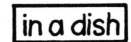 in a dish   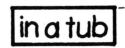 in a tub

GA1420

─oss

Write each of the letters below in front of ___ **oss** in each box. Draw a picture of each word. Cut out each box and glue the words in alphabetical order on a strip of paper.

b cr gl l m t

__oss	__oss	__oss
__oss	__oss	__oss

Toss is in the **oss** family.
You can toss lots of things.
Draw pictures of things you can toss on a sheet of paper.
Label each picture.

GA1420

-ot

Write each of the letters in front of ___ **ot** in each box. Draw a picture of each word.

c d h p kn p sp sh

___ot	___ot
___ot	___ot
___ot	___ot
___ot	___ot

Cut out the boxes below. Glue them on the back. Draw a picture.

lots of dots	hotshot	not hot	

GA1420

Long "A" Word Families

-ake
family

c_____   _____ake   _____   make

-ace
family

f_____   _____ace   _____   race

-ate
family

pl_____   _____ate   _____   state

-ape
family

_____   _____ape   _____   shape

If you have time, think of more words for these families. Write them on the back.

Long "E" (ee) Word Families

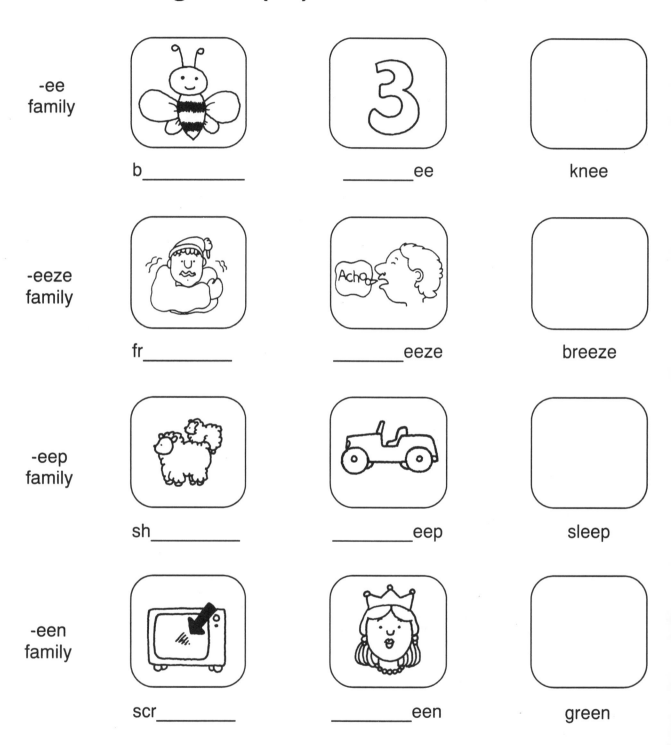

-ee
family

b_____   _____ee   knee

-eeze
family

fr_____   _____eeze   breeze

-eep
family

sh_____   _____eep   sleep

-een
family

scr_____   _____een   green

If you have time, think of more words for these families. Write them on the back.

GA1420

Long "O" Word Families

-one family

c_____

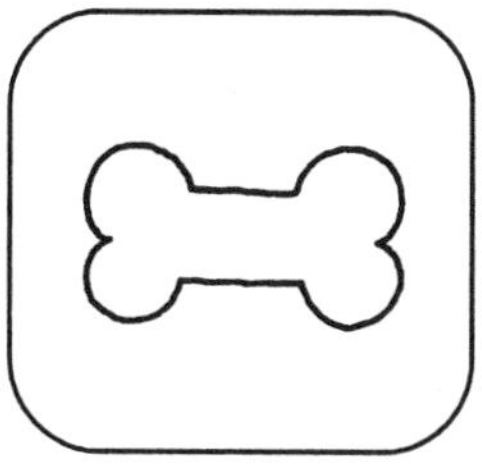

_____one

phone

-oke family

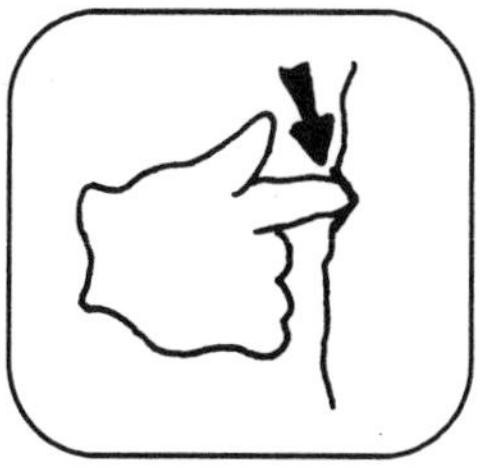

p_____

_____oke

choke

-ole family

h_____

_____ole

pole

-ose family

r_____

_____ose

close

If you have time, think of more words for these families. Write them on the back.

Long "I" Word Families

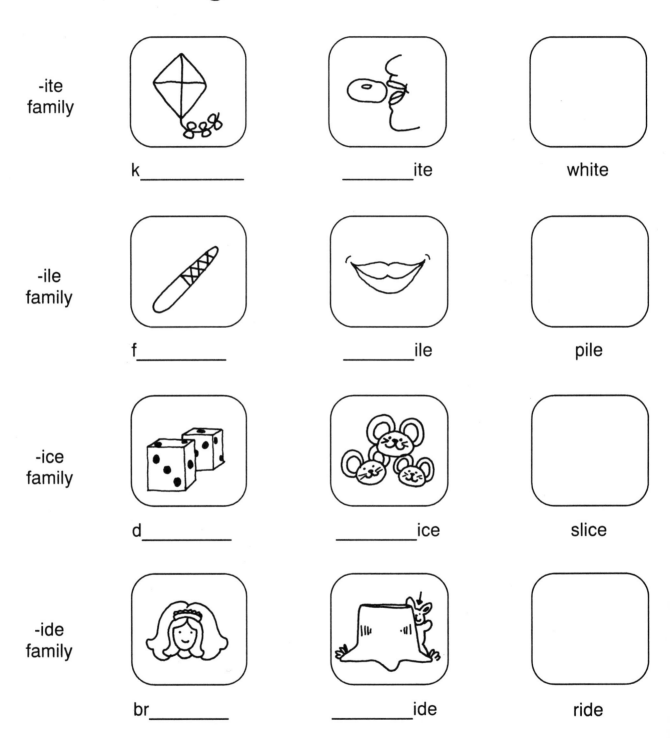

-ite family

k_____   _____ite   white

-ile family

f_____   _____ile   pile

-ice family

d_____   _____ice   slice

-ide family

br_____   _____ide   ride

If you have time, think of more words for these families. Write them on the back.

GA142

Long "A" (ai) Word Families

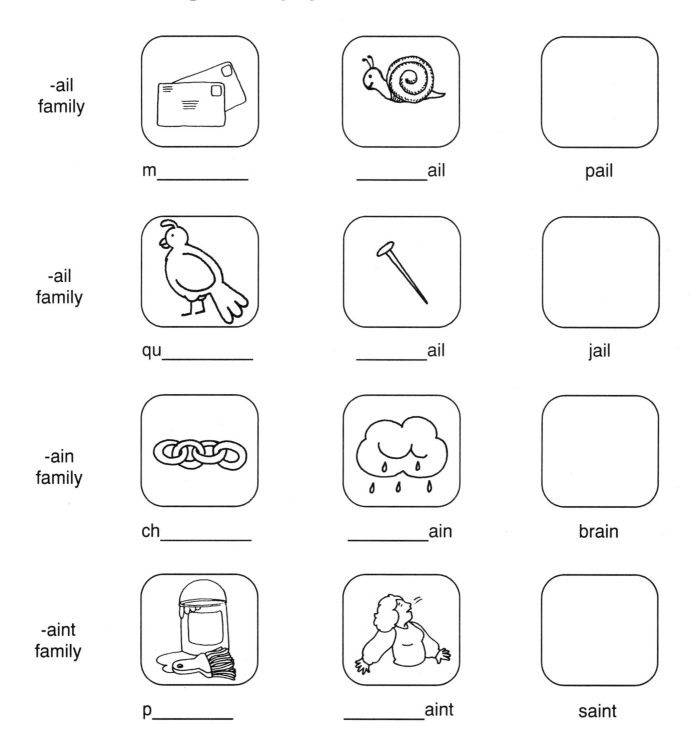

-ail
family

m_____   _____ail   pail

-ail
family

qu_____   _____ail   jail

-ain
family

ch_____   _____ain   brain

-aint
family

p_____   _____aint   saint

If you have time, think of more words for these families. Write them on the back.

GA1420

–and

Name _____

Write each of the letters below in front of ___ **and** in each box. Draw a picture of each word. Cut out each box and glue the words in alphabetical order on a strip of paper.

b   h   l   s   gr

__and	__and	__and
__and	__and	__and

Cut out the words below. Glue each to a scrap of paper. Draw pictures.

a cat and me	Mom and me	a dog and me

76

GA142

Word Families with Final "-ng"

-ing
family

k_____

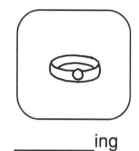

_____ing

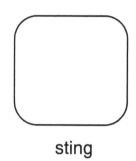

sting

-ang
family

f_____

_____ang

hang

-ong
family

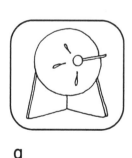

g_____

_____ong

long

If you have time, think of more words for these families. Write them on the back.

Word Families with Final "-nk"

-ank
family

b_____

_____ank

sank

-ink
family

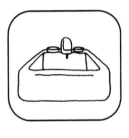

s_____

_____ink

pink

-unk
family

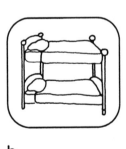

b_____

_____unk

junk

If you have time, think of more words for these families. Write them on the back.

GA142

–ing

Write each of the letters below in front of ___ ing in each box. Draw a picture of each word. Cut out each box and glue the words onto a piece of string. Hang from the ceiling.

k   s   w   r   st   sl

_ing	_ing	_ing
_ing	_ing	_ing

Make more **ing** words to add to your string. Try these letters: th   fl   p   str   br d.

GA1420

–ump

Write each of the letters below in front of ___ **ump** in each box. Draw a picture of each word. Cut out each box and glue the words in alphabetical order on a strip of paper.

b d h j l p

_ump	_ump	_ump
_ump	_ump	_ump

These words are in the **ump** family, too. Cut them out. Glue one word on the back of each box above. Draw a picture of each.

clump	grump	plump	slump

80

GA142

-ent

Write each of the letters below in front of ___ **ent** in each box. Draw a picture of each word.

b c d r s w

_ent	_ent	_ent
_ent	_ent	_ent

Cut out each word below. Glue each word to a corner on the back. Draw a picture of each word. Connect the picture to the correct word.

| scent | spent | vent | tent |

GA1420

-est

Write each of the letters below in front of ___ **est** in each box. Draw a picture of each word.

n   p   r   v   w   ch

_est	_est	_est
_est	_est	_est

Best is a word that ends in **est**.
On the back draw a picture of something you do best.
Write *best* at the bottom of the page.

GA1420

"OW" (cow) Word Families

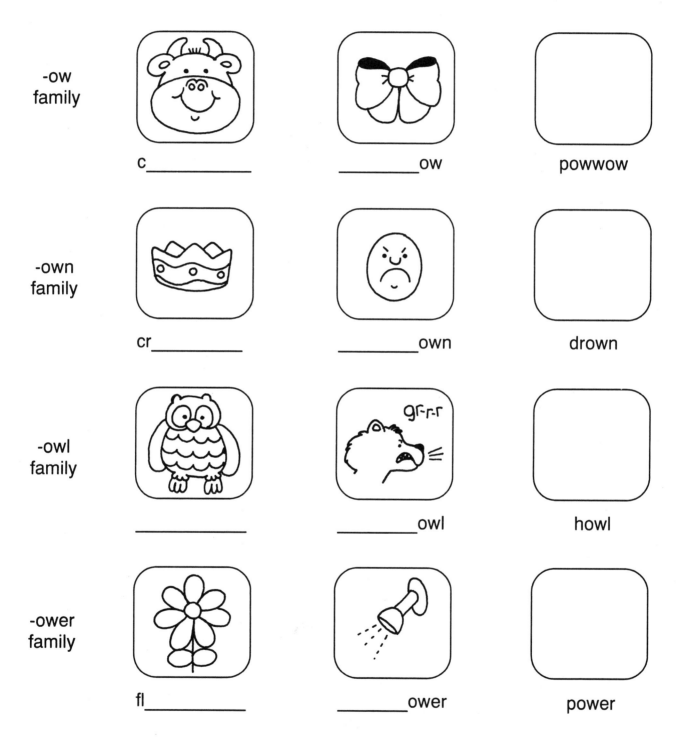

-ow family

c_____   _____ow   powwow

-own family

cr_____   _____own   drown

-owl family

_____   _____owl   howl

-ower family

fl_____   _____ower   power

If you have time, think of more words for these families. Write them on the back.

GA1420

"OO" (moon) Word Families

-oot
family

b_____   _____oot   shoot

-oom
family

bl_____   _____oom   boom

-oop
family

h_____   _____oop   droop

-oose
family

g_____   _____oose   loose

If you have time, think of more words for these families. Write them on the back.

GA1420

Writing Activities

We know that reading achievement and writing achievement are strongly and positively related. Beginning reading programs that emphasize writing activities have been shown to result in gains in reading achievement. Children who learn to read before entering school often begin writing first.

Writing forces children to convert speech sounds into letters. Phonics is the substitution of speech sounds for letters, the reverse process of writing. Reading and writing are, therefore, complementing skills. The following pages contain many writing activities for each of the letters of the alphabet and some letter combinations that produce unique sounds, such as **ch** and **th**.

The activities in this section are set up so that the teacher can cut them out, mount them and display them in a writing center or use them as extension activities throughout the day.

"A" Writing Activities

AAAAAAAAAAAAAAAAAAAAAAAAAAAAAAAAAAAAAAAAAAAAAAAAAAAA

a **On the Ads**
A Take one sheet of classified ads.
a Take one sheet of grocery ads.
A Turn the classified ads sideways.
a Make a list of groceries on the ads.
A
a **Materials**
A grocery ads
a classified ads
A crayons
a aaaaaaaaaaaaaaaaaaaaaaaaaaaaaaaaaaaaaaaaaaaaaaaaaaaaaaaa a

AAAAAAAAAAAAAAAAAAAAAAAAAAAAAAAAAAAAAAAAAAAAAAAAAAAA

a **Adding Machine Tape**
A Write an **a** word on a piece of adding machine tape.
a Draw a picture of the word.
A Make a vertical line before you write the next word.
a How long can you make your **a** list?
A
a
A **Materials**
a adding machine tape
A crayons
a aaaaaaaaaaaaaaaaaaaaaaaaaaaaaaaaaaaaaaaaaaaaaaaaaaaaaaaa a

AAAAAAAAAAAAAAAAAAAAAAAAAAAAAAAAAAAAAAAAAAAAAAAAAAAA

A Is for Animal
a Write *A Is for Animal* at the top of your paper.
A Write the names of different kinds of animals
a anywhere on the paper.
A Draw a picture of each animal on the paper.
a Draw a line to connect the two.
A
a
A **Materials**
a paper
A pencils
a crayons
A
a aaaaaaaaaaaaaaaaaaaaaaaaaaaaaaaaaaaaaaaaaaaaaaaaaaaaaaaa a

GA14

AAA

Alphabet Atlas

An atlas is a book that shows cities, states, countries, continents, lakes, rivers, oceans.

Find two friends to work with.

Name things you might see in an atlas.

Example: Washington, D.C.

Name as many things as you can.

Write the name of each on a square of paper.

Divide the squares up equally.

Illustrate each word.

Put all of the pictures in ABC order.

Staple them together.

Materials

atlas

6" x 6" (15.24 x 15.24 cm) squares of paper

pencils

crayons or markers

stapler

AAAAAAAAAAAAAAAAAAAAAAAAAAAAAAAAAAAAAAAAAAAAAAAAAAAAA

A Is for Addition

Fold your strip of paper into four boxes.

In the first box write about how many apples you have.

In the second box write about how many apples your friend has.

In the third box write about putting them together.

In the last box tell about how many you have in all.

Make up more addition problems in the same way.

Materials

4 1/2" x 18" (11.41 x 45.72 cm) paper

pencils or markers

GA1420

"B" Writing Activities

BBBBBBBBBBBBBBBBBBBBBBBBBBBBBBBBBBBBBBBBBBBBBBBBBBBBBBBB

B **Paper Grocery Bags** B

b Practice writing your uppercase and lowercase **Bb** on grocery bags with b
B crayons or water-soluble magic markers. B
b b
B Practice writing **b** words on the paper grocery bags. Write **b** words found in B
b grocery stores on the bags. Share your **b** words with classmates. b
B B
b Find pictures of objects that begin with the letter **b** in magazines and b
B catalogs and cut them out. Say the name of each object and write it on the B
b grocery bag. After you have written all your **b** words on the grocery bags, b
B put the pictures in the bag and take them home to share with your parents. B
b b
B **Materials** B
b paper grocery bags b
B crayons or water-soluble markers B
b magazines and catalogs b

bbbbbbbbbbbbbbbbbbbbbbbbbbbbbbbbbbbbbbbbbbbbbbbbbbbbbbbbbb

BBBBBBBBBBBBBBBBBBBBBBBBBBBBBBBBBBBBBBBBBBBBBBBBBBBBBBBB

B **B Is for Baby** B
b On a 3" x 5" (7.62 x 12.7 cm) index card make a list of words that name b
B baby clothes, furniture, behaviors, etc. Print the letters as small as you B
b can. b
B B
b **Materials** b
B 3" x 5" (7.62 x 12.7 cm) index cards B
b pencils b

bbbbbbbbbbbbbbbbbbbbbbbbbbbbbbbbbbbbbbbbbbbbbbbbbbbbbbbbbbbbbb

GA1420

BBB

Balloons

Blow up some balloons and write **b** words on them. Say the word on one of the balloons and then sit on the balloon until it pops.

Write the names of classmates and friends that begin with **b** on balloons. Take turns saying one of the names on a balloon and popping it by sticking it with the point of a pencil.

Materials
balloons
permanent markers
sharp pencils

bbbbbbbbbbbbbbbbbbbbbbbbbbbbbbbbbbbbbbbbbbbbbbbbbbbbbbbbbbbbbbbbbbbbb

BBBBBBBBBBBBBBBBBBBBBBBBBBBBBBBBBBBBBBBBBBBBBBBBBBBBBBBBBBBBBBBBB

Boxes

Cut pictures of **b** words from magazines and catalogs. Glue these pictures on all six sides of a box. Write the name of the object below each picture.

With wide line, water-soluble markers write the names of books you have read on the four sides of the box.

On a large box write all the words that name objects and animals that are bigger than you.

Materials
scissors
glue
water-soluble markers

bbbbbbbbbbbbbbbbbbbbbbbbbbbbbbbbbbbbbbbbbbbbbbbbbbbbbbbbbbbbbbbbbbbbb

BBBBBBBBBBBBBBBBBBBBBBBBBBBBBBBBBBBBBBBBBBBBBBBBBBBBBBBBBBBBBBBBB

B Is for Bicycle

Make a list of words that name bicycle parts on the page marked "Bicycle Words."

Materials
paper
pencils

bbbbbbbbbbbbbbbbbbbbbbbbbbbbbbbbbbbbbbbbbbbbbbbbbbbbbbbbbbbbbbbbbbbbb

GA1420

"C" Writing Activities

CCCCCCCCCCCCCCCCCCCCCCCCCCCCCCCCCCCCCCCCCCCCCCCCCCCCC

Colors on Construction Paper

Take a piece of construction paper.
Write the name of the color on the paper.
Do this with all the different colors of paper.
Put them in order and staple.
Make a cover.

Materials

strips of construction paper
black crayon or marker
stapler

ccccccccccccccccccccccccccccccccccccccccccccccccccccccccccc

CCCCCCCCCCCCCCCCCCCCCCCCCCCCCCCCCCCCCCCCCCCCCCCCCC

Calendars

Write the names of the days in the right boxes.
Write the name of the month at the top.
Draw some pictures on the edges.
Put the calendar in your desk or cubbie.
Write down special things you do each day.
Take it home at the end of the month.

Materials

blank calendar
pencils
crayons

ccccccccccccccccccccccccccccccccccccccccccccccccccccccccccc

CCCCCCCCCCCCCCCCCCCCCCCCCCCCCCCCCCCCCCCCCCCCCCCCCCCCC

Costs on Coupons

Write *coupon* at the top of your piece of paper.
Draw a picture of something you want to buy.
Write the amount of the coupon in each corner.
Make several.
Give some to a housekeeping area.

Materials

6" x 3" (15.24 x 7.62 cm) paper
crayons
pencils

ccccccccccccccccccccccccccccccccccccccccccccccccccccccccccc

GA142

CC

Cars

Write the name of a type of car on each piece of paper.
Put them in ABC order.
Staple together.

Materials

car-shaped sticky notes
pencils
stapler

CCCCCCCCCCCCCCCCCCCCCCCCCCCCCCCCCCCCCCCCCCCCCCCCCC

CCCCCCCCCCCCCCCCCCCCCCCCCCCCCCCCCCCCCCCCCCCCCCCCCC

Coins to Count

Sort your set of coins.
Fold a sheet of paper into four boxes.
Put a set of coins in each box.
Trace around all coins.
Put the coins back in the container.
Put the worth on each coin on your paper.
Add up the number of coins in each box.
Record the number. Example: 4 pennies

Materials

containers of coins (pennies, nickels, dimes, quarters)
paper
pencils

① ① ① ① ①	⑤ ⑤
5 pennies	2 nickels
⑩ ⑩ ⑩	㉕ ㉕ ㉕
3 dimes	3 quarters

CCCCCCCCCCCCCCCCCCCCCCCCCCCCCCCCCCCCCCCCCCCCCCCCCC

CCCCCCCCCCCCCCCCCCCCCCCCCCCCCCCCCCCCCCCCCCCCCCCCCC

Candy

Place your pieces of candy down the left-hand side of your paper.
Write the name of the candy next to it.
Put the candy back in the container.
Illustrate the candy next to the word.

Materials

containers of candy (wrapped)
paper
pencils
crayons

CCCCCCCCCCCCCCCCCCCCCCCCCCCCCCCCCCCCCCCCCCCCCCCCCC

GA1420

"D" Writing Activities

DDDDDDDDDDDDDDDDDDDDDDDDDDDDDDDDDDDDDDDDDDDDD

d **D Is for Days**
D Starting with Sunday, make a list of the names of the days of the week.
d
D **Materials**
d paper or blank calendar
D pencils
d ddddddddddddddddddddddddddddddddddddddddddddddddddddddd d

Sunday ...

DDDDDDDDDDDDDDDDDDDDDDDDDDDDDDDDDDDDDDDDDDDDD

d **D Is for Desk**
D Draw all the things that are in your desk.
d Label each of them.
D
d **Materials**
D paper
d pencils
D crayons
d ddddddddddddddddddddddddddddddddddddddddddddddddddddddd d

books   eraser crayons   pencils

DDDDDDDDDDDDDDDDDDDDDDDDDDDDDDDDDDDDDDDDDDDDD

d **D Is for Dairy**
D A dairy is a farm that produces milk and milk products.
d Make a list of dairy products or those foods made from milk.
D
d **Materials**
D paper
d pencils
D
d ddddddddddddddddddddddddddddddddddddddddddddddddddddddd d

DDDDDDDDDDDDDDDDDDDDDDDDDDDDDDDDDDDDDDDDDDDDD

d **D Is for Desserts**
D Make a list of a dozen desserts.
d Choose one of the desserts on your list.
D Write a story about why it is your favorite.
d
D **Materials**
d paper
D pencils
d ddddddddddddddddddddddddddddddddddddddddddddddddddddddd d

Apple Pie

GA1

DD

d **D Is for Dogs** d

Think of ten different kinds of dogs. Write one name on each piece of paper. Using books about dogs, mark the biggest kind of dog with the number 1 in the upper right-hand corner. Mark the paper containing the next biggest kind of dog with a number 2, and so on so that the paper with the name of the smallest kind of dog is marked with the number 10. Put a paper clip on your stack of papers.

Materials

3" x 5" (7.62 x 12.7 cm) pieces of paper

paper clips

books about kinds of dogs

POOdle

dddddddddddddddddddddddddddddddddddddddddddddddddddddddddddddd

DDDDDDDDDDDDDDDDDDDDDDDDDDDDDDDDDDDDDDDDDDDDDDDDDDDD

d **D Is for Dozen** d

How many are in a dozen?
Number your paper from 1 to 12.
Make a list of a dozen **d** words.
If it was easy, make a list of another dozen **d** words.

Materials

paper
pencils

1. dog   8.
2. daisy 9.
3. deer   10.
4. den   11.
5.   12.
6.
7.

dddddddddddddddddddddddddddddddddddddddddddddddddddddddddddddd

DDDDDDDDDDDDDDDDDDDDDDDDDDDDDDDDDDDDDDDDDDDDDDDDDDDD

d **D Is for Dinosaur** d

Make a list of a dozen dinosaurs.
Illustrate them.

Materials

books about dinosaurs
paper
pencils
crayons

dddddddddddddddddddddddddddddddddddddddddddddddddddddddddddddd

GA1420

"E" Writing Activities

EEEEEEEEEEEEEEEEEEEEEEEEEEEEEEEEEEEEEEEEEEEEEEEEEEEEEE

e **Everything with Ears**
E Listen carefully. What do you hear?
e Write down what you hear on a square of paper.
E Draw a picture of the word.
e Listen again. What else do you hear?
E
e **Materials**
E 6" x 6" (15.24 x 15.24 cm) squares of paper
e pencils
E crayons
e eeeeeeeeeeeeeeeeeeeeeeeeeeeeeeeeeeeeeeeeeeeeeeeeeeeee

EEEEEEEEEEEEEEEEEEEEEEEEEEEEEEEEEEEEEEEEEEEEEEEEEEEEEE

e **Environment**
E Find two friends to work with.
e Make a list of things in your environment. Write each thing on a separate
E small piece of paper.
e When you're finished, divide the pieces of paper.
E On a square of paper, illustrate the word.
e On a large sheet of paper, write how to take care of that part of the
E environment.
e Tape them all together.
E
e **Materials**
E 2" x 6" (5.08 x 15.24 cm) pieces of paper
e 6" x 6" (15.24" x 15.24" cm) pieces of paper
E 6" x 18" (15.24" x 45.72" cm) pieces of paper
e pencils
E crayons
e eeeeeeeeeeeeeeeeeeeeeeeeeeeeeeeeeeeeeeeeeeeeeeeeeeeee

EEEEEEEEEEEEEEEEEEEEEEEEEEEEEEEEEEEEEEEEEEEEEEEEEEEEEE

e **Enormous Elephants**
E Elephants are enormous. What else is enormous?
e Write the name of an enormous thing on the body of the elephant with
E black paint.
e
E **Materials**
E giant tempera-painted elephant
e black tempera
E brush
e eeeeeeeeeeeeeeeeeeeeeeeeeeeeeeeeeeeeeeeeeeeeeeeeeeeee

Gorilla

paint

GA142

EEE

e **Eleven Eggs**
E Take eleven egg shapes.
e Write an **e** word on the front side.
E Draw a picture of it on the back side.

When you have all eleven eggs done…
   Put them in ABC order.
   Mix them with a friend's eggs and put them all in ABC order.
   Turn them picture-side up. Place along a sheet of paper. Write the word
   for each next to the egg.

Materials
eleven egg shapes per child
crayons
dictionaries
pencils
eeeeeeeeeeeeeeeeeeeeeeeeeeeeeeeeeeeeeeeeeeeeeeeeee

EEEEEEEEEEEEEEEEEEEEEEEEEEEEEEEEEEEEEEEEEEEEEEEEE

e **Eggs of Plastic**
E Write **e** words on strips of paper.
e Copy the **e** words onto the plastic egg.
E Place the strips in the egg.

Materials
one plastic egg per child,
small strips of paper
permanent markers or crayons
eeeeeeeeeeeeeeeeeeeeeeeeeeeeeeeeeeeeeeeeeeeeeeeeee

EEEEEEEEEEEEEEEEEEEEEEEEEEEEEEEEEEEEEEEEEEEEEEEEE

e **Elementary School on an Easel**
E Go outside and take a good look at your elementary school.
e Paint a picture of your elementary school.
E Write the name of it across the top.

Materials
easel
tempera paint
18" x 24" (45.72 x 60.96 cm) sheets of paper
eeeeeeeeeeeeeeeeeeeeeeeeeeeeeeeeeeeeeeeeeeeeeeeeee

GA1420

"F" Writing Activities

FFFFFFFFFFFFFFFFFFFFFFFFFFFFFFFFFFFFFFFFFFFFFFFFFFFFFFFFFFFFFFFF

F Is for File Folder

On the outside of a file folder, make a list of feelings, such as love, sadness, joy, peace, etc.

On the inside of the file folder, name a person you know and tell why you love or like him/her.

Materials

file folders

pencils

ffffffffffffffffffffffffffffffffffffffffffffffffffffffffffffffffffffffffffffffffffffffffff

FFFFFFFFFFFFFFFFFFFFFFFFFFFFFFFFFFFFFFFFFFFFFFFFFFFFF

F Is for Fast Foods

Make a list of your favorite fast foods on a file folder. Write those that are made from meat with a brown marker. Use a green marker for those that are made from potatoes or onions. Use a red marker for the fast foods that are desserts.

Materials

file folders

markers (brown, green and red)

ffffffffffffffffffffffffffffffffffffffffffffffffffffffffffffffffffffffffffffffffffffffffff

FFFFFFFFFFFFFFFFFFFFFFFFFFFFFFFFFFFFFFFFFFFFFFFFFFFF

F Is for Famous

On a file folder, make a list of famous people.

Find a classmate and tell him/her why each person is famous.

Materials

file folders

pencils

ffffffffffffffffffffffffffffffffffffffffffffffffffffffffffffffffffffffffffffffffffffffffff

FFFFFFFFFFFFFFFFFFFFFFFFFFFFFFFFFFFFFFFFFFFFFFFFFFFFF

F Is for Fear

On a file folder, write a story about something that caused fear in you.

Materials

file folders

pencils

ffffffffffffffffffffffffffffffffffffffffffffffffffffffffffffffffffffffffffffffffffffffffff

GA142

FFF

F Is for Fingers

On the outside of a file folder, draw the outline of one of your hands with the fingers spread apart. On the inside of the file folder, make a list of all the things you can pick up with your fingers.

Materials
file folders
pencils

FFFFFFFFFFFFFFFFFFFFFFFFFFFFFFFFFFFFFFFFFFFFFFFFFFFFFFFFFFFFFFFFFFFFFFFFF

F Is for Fill

On the outside of a file folder, make a list of the things you can fill and with what you can fill them. For example, you can fill a cup with milk, juice, water, hot chocolate, tea, or cider. On the inside of the file folder, draw pictures of some of the things with which you like to fill your stomach. Label each item you draw with its name.

Materials
file folders
markers
crayons

FFFFFFFFFFFFFFFFFFFFFFFFFFFFFFFFFFFFFFFFFFFFFFFFFFFFFFFFFFFFFFFFFFFFFFFFF

F Is for Feathers

On the outside of a file folder, write the word *feathers* in large letters. Now open the file folder. On the page to the left, draw and label animals that have feathers. On the right page draw and label those things that are made from feathers.

Materials
file folders
markers or crayons
a feather to look at
books about feathers and animals that have feathers

Feathers

97

GA1420

"G" Writing Activities

GGGGGGGGGGGGGGGGGGGGGGGGGGGGGGGGGGGGGGGGGGGGGGG

Grocery Lists

Find a friend to work with.

One person takes the paper and pencil.

Both of you think of things to get at the grocery store.

Write them all down on the list.

Write down the costs from the ads.

How much do you think your groceries will cost?

eggs 80¢
milk 1.25
juice 1.50

Materials

paper

pencils

grocery ads

ggggggggggggggggggggggggggggggggggggggggggggggggggggggggggggggg

GGGGGGGGGGGGGGGGGGGGGGGGGGGGGGGGGGGGGGGGGGGGGGG

Garbage

Shape your green paper into a garbage can.

Look at all the garbage in the garbage can.

Write down all the things you see onto your can.

Write the date and your name on the can.

Give this to your teacher to save.

paper
banana peel

Materials

9" x 12" (22.86 x 30.48 cm) green paper

scissors

crayons

pencils

yesterday's garbage (trash) can

Note: Do this three to four times a year. Go back after the last time and try to remember what was done each day before by examining the garbage.

ggggggggggggggggggggggggggggggggggggggggggggggggggggggggggggggg

GGGGGGGGGGGGGGGGGGGGGGGGGGGGGGGGGGGGGGGGGGGGGGG

Gutter

Take paper and pencil outside.

Go see what's in the gutter. Write it down.

nickel
old shoe

Materials

paper

pencils

ggggggggggggggggggggggggggggggggggggggggggggggggggggggggggggggg

GG

Gum

Write the name of a kind of gum on each strip.
Decorate the strip to look like the real gum.

Materials

gum wrapper-sized strips of paper
pencils
crayons
sample wrappers

ggggggggggggggggggggggggggggggggggggggggggggggggggg

GGGGGGGGGGGGGGGGGGGGGGGGGGGGGGGGGGGGGGGGGGGGGGGGGG

Garden

Paint or draw a picture of a garden.
Let the picture dry.
Write the name of each thing in your garden on a Popsicle stick.
Glue the stick near the plant in your picture.

Materials

Popsicle sticks
paints or crayons
paper
glue

ggggggggggggggggggggggggggggggggggggggggggggggggggg

GGGGGGGGGGGGGGGGGGGGGGGGGGGGGGGGGGGGGGGGGGGGGGGGGG

Greeting Cards

Look at all of the cards in the center.
Design a greeting card to send to a friend.
Take it home for your parents to address.

Materials

sample greeting cards
folded sheets of paper
crayons or markers
pencils

ggggggggggggggggggggggggggggggggggggggggggggggggggg

GGGGGGGGGGGGGGGGGGGGGGGGGGGGGGGGGGGGGGGGGGGGGGGGGG

Games

What is your favorite game?
Write and illustrate the directions for the game.

Materials

paper
pencils
crayons

ggggggggggggggggggggggggggggggggggggggggggggggggggg

GA1420

"H" Writing Activities

HHHHHHHHHHHHHHHHHHHHHHHHHHHHHHHHHHHHHHHHHHHHHHHHHHHHHHHHH

H Is for Hamburger

Cut two round shapes from manila construction paper. These shapes will be the top and bottom of the hamburger bun.

Label the word *bun* on them.

Cut a round shape from brown construction paper.

Write the word *hamburger* on it.

Use another brown round shape if you want to make it a double burger.

Cut out other shapes from construction paper to add other things to your hamburger.

Label each.

When you are finished making your hamburger, staple it together with only one staple near the top side of the hamburger.

Materials

construction paper (red, manila, brown, white, green, and yellow)

markers

scissors

stapler

hhhhhhhhhhhhhhhhhhhhhhhhhhhhhhhhhhhhhhhhhhhhhhhhhhhhhhhhhhhhhh

HHHHHHHHHHHHHHHHHHHHHHHHHHHHHHHHHHHHHHHHHHHHHHHHHHHHHHHH

H Is for Handles

On a blank sheet of paper make a list of those objects that have handles.

Illustrate your paper by drawing some objects with handles.

hhhhhhhhhhhhhhhhhhhhhhhhhhhhhhhhhhhhhhhhhhhhhhhhhhhhhhhhhhhhhhhhhh

HHHHHHHHHHHHHHHHHHHHHHHHHHHHHHHHHHHHHHHHHHHHHHHHHHHHHHHH

H Is for Hundred

Number your paper from 1 to 100. Make a list of a hundred words that either begin with the letter **h** or words that have the letter **h** in them.

hhhhhhhhhhhhhhhhhhhhhhhhhhhhhhhhhhhhhhhhhhhhhhhhhhhhhhhhhhhhhhhhhh

GA142

HHH

H Is for Hands

Draw the outline of your left hand with the fingers spread apart on a blank sheet of paper.

Cut out the shape of your left hand.

Now draw the outline of your right hand on a blank sheet of paper.

Cut out this shape, too.

Make a list of the things you can do with your hands on one side of the shapes of your left and right hands.

Glue these two shapes together so that the words are on the outside.

Materials

blank paper

pencils

scissors

glue

hhhhhhhhhhhhhhhhhhhhhhhhhhhhhhhhhhhhhhhhhhhhhhhhhhhhhhhhhhhh

HHHHHHHHHHHHHHHHHHHHHHHHHHHHHHHHHHHHHHHHHHHHHHHHHHHHHHH

H Is for Head

Make a list of the things people wear on their heads.

Illustrate each one.

Materials

paper

pencils

crayons

hhhhhhhhhhhhhhhhhhhhhhhhhhhhhhhhhhhhhhhhhhhhhhhhhhhhhhhhhhhh

HHHHHHHHHHHHHHHHHHHHHHHHHHHHHHHHHHHHHHHHHHHHHHHHHHHHHHH

H Is for Holiday

Look at all of the holidays marked on a calendar.

Choose your favorite two holidays and on a sheet of paper tell why you like them.

Materials

calendar with all the holidays marked

blank paper

pencils

hhhhhhhhhhhhhhhhhhhhhhhhhhhhhhhhhhhhhhhhhhhhhhhhhhhhhhhhhhhh

GA1420

"I" Writing Activities

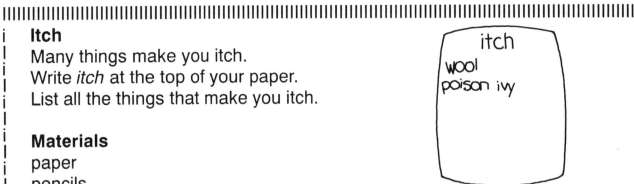

Itch

Many things make you itch.
Write *itch* at the top of your paper.
List all the things that make you itch.

Materials

paper
pencils

Ivory

Take a piece of ivory paper.
Go around the room to find ivory things.
Record the names on the sheet of ivory paper.
Draw pictures for each at your table or desk.
Cut out all the ivory things.
Glue each to brown paper.
Label each.

Materials

manila (ivory) paper
brown paper
scissors
pencils
crayons or markers
glue

Ice Cream

Find two friends. Choose one to write.
On each ice-cream carton shape, write the name of one kind of ice cream.
Divide up the cartons. Illustrate them.
Put them up in the room for everyone to see.

Materials

carton-shaped paper
crayons
pencils

GA14

Ill

Being ill is never fun.
Draw a picture of a sad, ill face.
Glue on a thermometer.
Make a list of **ill** words on the thermometer.

Materials
8 1/2" (21.6 cm) paper
crayons
2" x 8" (5.08 x 20.32 cm) paper (for thermometer)
sample thermometer
pencils

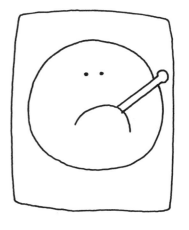

Ice Box

Some people call refrigerators ice boxes.
Tape two sheets of white paper together at the edge to make the ice box.
Cut out things from the grocery ads that go in an ice box.
Glue them in your ice box.
Label each one.

Materials
tape
two pieces 8 1/2" (21.6 cm) white paper per child
grocery ads
scissors
glue
pencils

Igloo

Make an igloo out of white paper.
On the back list things you find in an igloo.
Draw a picture for each.
Check with a friend to see what's in his igloo.
Add some things to yours if you want.

Materials
white paper
pencils
crayons

GA1420

"J" Writing Activities

JJJJJJJJJJJJJJJJJJJJJJJJJJJJJJJJJJJJJJJJJJJJJJJJJJJJJJJJJJJJJJJJJJJJJJJJJJJJJJJJJJ

J Is for Jump

On a 3" x 5" (7.62 x 12.7 cm) piece of paper, write one object you can jump over. Write as many things that you can jump over on other sheets in the same way.

When you are finished, put the sheets in order beginning with the smallest object and ending with the biggest or tallest object or thing.

Materials

3" x 5" (7.62 x 12.7 cm) pieces of paper
pencil

tennis ball | basket-ball | sand-box

jjjjjjjjjjjjjjjjjjjjjjjjjjjjjjjjjjjjjjjjjjjjjjjjjjjjjjjjjjjjjjjjjjjjjjjjjjjjjjjjjjjjjjjjj

JJJJJJJJJJJJJJJJJJJJJJJJJJJJJJJJJJJJJJJJJJJJJJJJJJJJJJJJJJJJJJJJJJJJJJJJJJJJJJJJJJ

J Is for January, June and July

Three months of the year begin with the letter **j**. Write these months across the top of a blank sheet of paper. Under the name of each month, write the things you can play or do. Circle the things that can be done inside. Draw a line under the things that can be done outside. Put a check (√) after the things that can be done inside and outside.

jjjjjjjjjjjjjjjjjjjjjjjjjjjjjjjjjjjjjjjjjjjjjjjjjjjjjjjjjjjjjjjjjjjjjjjjjjjjjjjjjjjjjjjjj

JJJJJJJJJJJJJJJJJJJJJJJJJJJJJJJJJJJJJJJJJJJJJJJJJJJJJJJJJJJJJJJJJJJJJJJJJJJJJJJJJJ

J Is for Jungle

Make a list of animals that live in a jungle. Draw a picture of the smallest and the biggest animal on your list. Print the name of the animal under it.

Materials

paper
pencils
markers or crayons
books about jungle animals

Parrot   elephant

jjjjjjjjjjjjjjjjjjjjjjjjjjjjjjjjjjjjjjjjjjjjjjjjjjjjjjjjjjjjjjjjjjjjjjjjjjjjjjjjjjjjjjjjj

GA142

JJJ

J Is for Jet

A jet is a type or kind of airplane. Look at the airplane book and see what a jet looks like. Draw a jet on your paper and label the parts of the plane.

Materials

paper
pencils
books about planes that include pictures of jets

jjjjjjjjjjjjjjjjjjjjjjjjjjjjjjjjjjjjjjjjjjjjjjjjjjjjjjjjjjjjjjjjjjjjjjjjjjjjjjjjjjjjjjjjjjjjjjjjj

JJJJJJJJJJJJJJJJJJJJJJJJJJJJJJJJJJJJJJJJJJJJJJJJJJJJJJJJJJJJJJJJJJJJJJJJJJJJJ

J Is for Juice

Make a list of all the different kinds of juices that you have tried. Beside each one draw a picture of the fruit from which it comes.

jjjjjjjjjjjjjjjjjjjjjjjjjjjjjjjjjjjjjjjjjjjjjjjjjjjjjjjjjjjjjjjjjjjjjjjjjjjjjjjjjjjjjjjjjjjjjjjjj

JJJJJJJJJJJJJJJJJJJJJJJJJJJJJJJJJJJJJJJJJJJJJJJJJJJJJJJJJJJJJJJJJJJJJJJJJJJJJ

J Is for Jack-o'-lantern

Draw a picture of a jack-o'-lantern with a happy face. Write the word *happy* beside it. Now draw a picture of a jack-o'-lantern with a sad face. Write the word *sad* beside it. Finally draw a picture of a jack-o'-lantern with another kind of face. Write a word beside it that tells about this jack-o'-lantern's face.

jjjjjjjjjjjjjjjjjjjjjjjjjjjjjjjjjjjjjjjjjjjjjjjjjjjjjjjjjjjjjjjjjjjjjjjjjjjjjjjjjjjjjjjjjjjjjjjjj

JJJJJJJJJJJJJJJJJJJJJJJJJJJJJJJJJJJJJJJJJJJJJJJJJJJJJJJJJJJJJJJJJJJJJJJJJJJJJ

J Is for Journey

A journey is a trip. Write a story telling about a journey you took with your family. Be sure to tell where you went and what you did while you were there.

jjjjjjjjjjjjjjjjjjjjjjjjjjjjjjjjjjjjjjjjjjjjjjjjjjjjjjjjjjjjjjjjjjjjjjjjjjjjjjjjjjjjjjjj

GA1420

"K" Writing Activities

KKKKKKKKKKKKKKKKKKKKKKKKKKKKKKKKKKKKKKKKKKKKKKKKKKKKKKKKKKKKKK

Kindergarten

Write *kindergarten* at the top of your paper.

Make a list of things you do in kindergarten.

Write the word and draw the picture.

Share the list with other children who are coming to kindergarten next year.

Materials

paper

pencils

crayons

kkkkkkkkkkkkkkkkkkkkkkkkkkkkkkkkkkkkkkkkkkkkkkkkkkkkkkkkkkkkkkkkkkkkk

KKKKKKKKKKKKKKKKKKKKKKKKKKKKKKKKKKKKKKKKKKKKKKKKKKKKKKKKKKKKKK

K Words on a Kite

Make a kite by cutting off the corners of the paper.

Decorate your kite.

Glue small strips to some string to make a tail.

Write **k** words on the *tail* of the kite.

Materials

12" x 18" (30.48 x 45.72 cm) sheet of paper per child

crayons

yarn

2" x 6" (5.08 x 15.24 cm) strips for tail

kkkkkkkkkkkkkkkkkkkkkkkkkkkkkkkkkkkkkkkkkkkkkkkkkkkkkkkkkkkkkkkkkkkk

KKKKKKKKKKKKKKKKKKKKKKKKKKKKKKKKKKKKKKKKKKKKKKKKKKKKKKKKKKKKKK

K Is for Kansas. K Is for Kentucky.

Look at a map of the United States.

Write *Kansas* at the top of a sheet of paper.

Make a list of all the things you see in Kansas.

Write *Kentucky* at the top of a sheet of paper.

Make a list of all the things you see in Kentucky.

Materials

state-shaped pieces of paper

pencils

kkkkkkkkkkkkkkkkkkkkkkkkkkkkkkkkkkkkkkkkkkkkkkkkkkkkkkkkkkkkkkkkkkkkk

GA142

KKK

Kitchen

Look in a catalog.
What goes in a kitchen?
Cut out the pictures.
Write *kitchen* at the top of a sheet of paper.
Glue pictures of kitchen things onto a sheet of paper.
Label each one.

Materials

catalogs
scissors
glue
pencils
paper

kkkkkkkkkkkkkkkkkkkkkkkkkkkkkkkkkkkkkkkkkkkkkkkkkkkkkkkkkkkkkkkkkkkkkkkkkkk

KKKKKKKKKKKKKKKKKKKKKKKKKKKKKKKKKKKKKKKKKKKKKKKKKKKKKKKKKKKKKKK

Ketchup

Write *ketchup* on each red strip.
On the back write *Ketchup goes on* _____.
Fill in the blank.
Do as many different ones as you can.
Read them to a friend.

Ketchup goes on hamburgers.

Materials

3" x 9" (7.62 x 22.86 cm) red strips
pencils

kkkkkkkkkkkkkkkkkkkkkkkkkkkkkkkkkkkkkkkkkkkkkkkkkkkkkkkkkkkkkkkkkkkkkkkkkkk

KKKKKKKKKKKKKKKKKKKKKKKKKKKKKKKKKKKKKKKKKKKKKKKKKKKKKKKKKKKKKKK

Kids in My Class

Put your name on a sheet of paper at the top.
Ask each kid in your class to sign your paper.
Cut out all of the names.
Put them in ABC order.
Make a new list that shows them in ABC order.

Mindy

Materials

two sheets of paper per child
pencils
scissors

kkkkkkkkkkkkkkkkkkkkkkkkkkkkkkkkkkkkkkkkkkkkkkkkkkkkkkkkkkkkkkkkkkkkkkkkkkk

GA1420

"L" Writing Activities

LLLLLLLLLLLLLLLLLLLLLLLLLLLLLLLLLLLLLLLLLLLLLLLLLLLLLLLLLLLLLLLLLLLLLLLLL
I **L Is for Liquid**
L Make a list of all the things that are liquid.
I For example, water and milk are liquids.
IIIIIIIIIIIIIIIIIIIIIIIIIIIIIIIIIIIIIIIIIIIIIIIIIIIIIIIIIIIIIIIIIIIIIIIIIIIIIIIII

LLLLLLLLLLLLLLLLLLLLLLLLLLLLLLLLLLLLLLLLLLLLLLLLLLLLLLLLLLLLLLLLLLLLLLLLL
I **L Is for Level**
L Make a list of things that are level or flat.
I For example, the floor of the classroom is level or flat.
IIIIIIIIIIIIIIIIIIIIIIIIIIIIIIIIIIIIIIIIIIIIIIIIIIIIIIIIIIIIIIIIIIIIIIIIIIIIIIIII

LLLLLLLLLLLLLLLLLLLLLLLLLLLLLLLLLLLLLLLLLLLLLLLLLLLLLLLLLLLLLLLLLLLLLLLLL
I **L Is for List**
L Mothers and fathers usually go to the grocery store with a list of things to L
I buy.
L Make a list of groceries for your mother to buy at the store.
I Make a list of things you own or are in your bedroom at home.
IIIIIIIIIIIIIIIIIIIIIIIIIIIIIIIIIIIIIIIIIIIIIIIIIIIIIIIIIIIIIIIIIIIIIIIIIIIIIIIII

LLLLLLLLLLLLLLLLLLLLLLLLLLLLLLLLLLLLLLLLLLLLLLLLLLLLLLLLLLLLLLLLLLLLLLLLL
I **L Is for Like**
L Fold your paper in half. Now fold it in half again. Open the paper. Your L
I paper should have four rows. At the top of the row on the left write *People I* I
L *Like* and draw a line under it. At the top of the next row write *Foods I Like* L
I and draw a line under it. Write *Things I Like to Do* at the top of the third row I
L and draw a line under it. Write *People Who Like Me* at the top of the row on L
I the right and draw a line under it. Now write a list of words and names that I
L go in each row.
IIIIIIIIIIIIIIIIIIIIIIIIIIIIIIIIIIIIIIIIIIIIIIIIIIIIIIIIIIIIIIIIIIIIIIIIIIIIIIIII

GA14

LLL

L Is for Lampshade

In your best handwriting, print your full name on the classroom lampshade.
Below your name write your date of birth.

Materials

Lampshade that has a smooth shade and markers that will write on it.

LLLLLLLLLLLLLLLLLLLLLLLLLLLLLLLLLLLLLLLLLLLLLLLLLLLLLLLLLLLLLLLLLLL

L Is for Lunch

Make a lunch box out of construction paper.
Make some of your favorite foods.
Label them.
Put them in your lunch box.

Materials

construction paper
pencils
scissors
glue

LLLLLLLLLLLLLLLLLLLLLLLLLLLLLLLLLLLLLLLLLLLLLLLLLLLLLLLLLLLLLLLLLLL

L Is for Letters

Write a letter to your mom and dad telling them what you are learning in school today.
Take the letter home and give it to them.

Materials

pencils
stationery
envelopes

Mom and Dad

LLLLLLLLLLLLLLLLLLLLLLLLLLLLLLLLLLLLLLLLLLLLLLLLLLLLLLLLLLLLLLLLLLL

L Is for Left

Make a list of all the things you can do with your left hand.

left

GA1420

"M" Writing Activities

MMMMMMMMMMMMMMMMMMMMMMMMMMMMMMMMMMMMMMMMMMMMMM

m **Magic Magnets**   m
M Test each object in the box with a magnet.   M
m Put the ones that stick to the magnet in one pile.   m
M At the top of a sheet of paper write *magnets*.   M
m Write the name of each thing that sticks.   m
M Draw a picture of it next to it.   M
m **Materials**   m
M magnet   M
m box of objects   m
M paper   M
m pencils   m
M crayons   M
m mmmmmmmmmmmmmmmmmmmmmmmmmmmmmmmmmmmmmmmmmmmmm m

MMMMMMMMMMMMMMMMMMMMMMMMMMMMMMMMMMMMMMMMMMMMMM

m **Money**   m
M Look closely at a penny.   M
   Make a large tan circle.   m
m Write the words from the penny on the circle.   M
M Do the same for a nickel, dime and quarter on gray paper.   m
m **Materials**   M
M penny, nickel, dime, quarter   m
m tan and gray paper   M
M 6" (15.24 cm), 8" (20.32 cm) and 9" (22.86 cm) circles   m
m patterns   M
M pencils   m
m mmmmmmmmmmmmmmmmmmmmmmmmmmmmmmmmmmmmmmmmmmmmm m

MMMMMMMMMMMMMMMMMMMMMMMMMMMMMMMMMMMMMMMMMMMMMM

m **Marvelous Moms**   m
M At the bottom of each sheet of paper write *Moms can* _____. M
m Fill in the blank with something Moms can do.   m
M Draw a picture for each one.   M
m Put them all together. Staple and make a cover.   m
M **Materials**   M
m 6" x 6" (15.24 x 15.24 cm) paper   m
M crayons   M
m pencils   m
m stapler   m
M construction paper for covers   M
m mmmmmmmmmmmmmmmmmmmmmmmmmmmmmmmmmmmmmmmmmmmmm m

GA142

M MMMMMMMMMMMMMMMMMMMMMMMMMMMMMMMMMMMMMMMMMMMMMMM M

Menu

Make a list of things you like to eat.
Put a price next to each one.
Write *Menu* at the top of your sheet.
Design a cover for your menu that has your name on it.
Tape the cover to the menu along the left edge.
Ask a friend to make a list of things to eat from your menu.

Materials
paper
pencils
crayons
tape

m mmmmmmmmmmmmmmmmmmmmmmmmmmmmmmmmmmmmmmmmmmmm m

M MMMMMMMMMMMMMMMMMMMMMMMMMMMMMMMMMMMMMMMMMMMM M

Males

Make a list of the males in your class.
Cut the names out.
Put them in ABC order.
Rewrite the list.

Materials
paper
pencils
scissors

m mmmmmmmmmmmmmmmmmmmmmmmmmmmmmmmmmmmmmmmmmmmm m

M MMMMMMMMMMMMMMMMMMMMMMMMMMMMMMMMMMMMMMMMMMMMM M

Monsters

Draw a picture of a monster.
Write scary words on the edges of the paper.

Materials
paper
crayons
pencils

m mmmmmmmmmmmmmmmmmmmmmmmmmmmmmmmmmmmmmmmmmmmmm m

M MMMMMMMMMMMMMMMMMMMMMMMMMMMMMMMMMMMMMMMMMMMMMM M

Mud

Mix some mud outside.
Spread it on the ground.
Make **m** words in the mud.

Materials
dirt
water

m mmmmmmmmmmmmmmmmmmmmmmmmmmmmmmmmmmmmmmmmmmmm m

GA1420

"N" Writing Activities

N NNNNNNNNNNNNNNNNNNNNNNNNNNNNNNNNNNNNNNNNNNNNNNN N
n **N Is for Noodles**
N Make ten words with alphabet noodles that begin with the letter **n**.
n Make ten more words that have the letter **n** at the end.
N Spell ten of your classmates' names with the alphabet noodles.
n
N **Materials**
n alphabet noodles
N nnnnnnnnnnnnnnnnnnnnnnnnnnnnnnnnnnnnnnnnnnnnnnnnnn

NAIL NINE TIN ANGLE

N NNNNNNNNNNNNNNNNNNNNNNNNNNNNNNNNNNNNNNNNNNNNNN N
n **N Is for Names and Numbers**
N Write the names of ten of your class-
n mates on 3" x 5" (7.62 x 12.7 cm)
N sheets of paper with one name on each
n sheet of paper. Add their birth day
N (month, day, and year) below each
n name. Now put the names in alphabet-
N ical order.
n
N Take these same papers and put them
n in order by age with the youngest first.
N
n Make a list of boy and girl names that
N begin with the letter **n**. Circle the girl
n names. Draw a line under the boy
N names.
n
N **Materials**
n ten 3" x 5" (7.62 x 12.7 cm) sheets of
N paper
n book of boy and girl names
N nnnnnnnnnnnnnnnnnnnnnnnnnnnnnnnnnnnnnnnnnnnnnnnnn n

Tiffany Jones
January 10th, 1985

Nathan
Nick
Natalie
Nelly
Norman
Nora

GA14

NN

N Is for Notebook

A notebook has several sheets of paper that are held together with a cover and back. Take nine half sheets of paper and put a half sheet of construction paper on the top and one on the bottom. Staple the top left corner and the bottom left corner. Now you have your own notebook for making notes. On the cover write "This notebook belongs to _____." and write your name.

At the top of the first three pages write the word *Names*. Write some of your relatives, friends, and classmates' names. Write a note beside each name. For example, you could write, "my best friend," or "tallest girl in my class."

At the top of the next three pages write the word *Numbers*. Write notes about numbers in your class. For example, you could tell how many classmates you have. How many are boys and how many are girls? Write the name and age of the oldest classmate. Write the name and height of the tallest classmate. Write the names and birthdays of your classmates that were born in the ninth month of the year. What other numbers can you make notes about?

At the top of the last three pages write the word *Nicknames*. Make a list of your friends and write their nicknames beside their names.

Materials

half sheets of paper
construction paper
stapler

nnnnnnnnnnnnnnnnnnnnnnnnnnnnnnnnnnnnnnnnnnnnnnnnnnnnnn

GA1420

"O" Writing Activities

October

October is fun month. Many things happen.

Write *October* at the top of the orange paper.

Write October words on your paper.

Draw pictures of each word with your pencil on some black paper.

Cut out each illustration and glue it on your orange paper.

Materials

orange paper

black paper

pencils

scissors

glue

Orchestra

An orchestra is made up of many instruments.

Draw a picture of the different instruments you know are in an orchestra.

Label each picture.

Materials

paper

pencils

crayons

Orange

On each piece of orange paper write the word of something that is orange.

Draw a black picture on each word card.

Materials

6" x 6" (15.24 x 15.24 cm) squares of orange paper

pencils

black crayons

GA1420

Outside

Look outside the window.
Draw a picture of what you see.
Label each part.

Materials

paper

crayons

pencils

Oval

Many things are oval in shape.
Make each oval shape into something that is oval.
Write the name of what it is on the back.
Find a friend who is finished, too.
Hold up your oval thing and let your friend try to guess what it is.
Do the same thing with your friend's oval thing.

Materials

several ovals per child

crayons

pencils

O'Clock

Make a TV set from the materials.
Glue the white sheet onto the brown sheet for a screen.
Draw some knobs.
Make a list of TV shows that come on at each time during the day.
Write the sentence like this: 9 o'clock   Sesame Street

Materials

9" x 12" (22.86 x 30.48 cm) brown construction paper

7" x 8" (17.78 x 20.32 cm) white paper

crayons

pencils

glue

GA1420

"P" Writing Activities

P PPPPPPPPPPPPPPPPPPPPPPPPPPPPPPPPPPPPPPPPPPPPPPP P

P Is for Paper Plate

Fold a paper plate in half and with scissors cut along the fold. Take one of the halves and put it against another paper plate. The tops should be facing each other. Staple these together by stapling along the edges of the two plates. You have just made a paper plate pocket. Write your name on the whole paper plate.

On 3" x 5" (7.62 x 12.7 cm) sheets of paper write words that begin with the letter **p**. Write one word only on each sheet of paper. When you finish, staple the sheets with one staple in the top left corner. Put these in your paper plate pocket.

Give a 3" x 5" (7.62 x 12.7 cm) sheet of paper to five classmates and ask them to write a math problem on the paper. Solve the problems and put the sheets in your paper plate pocket.

Write a poem with a pen or pencil on a half sheet of paper. Read this poem to a person in your class. Then fold the paper in half and put it in your paper plate pocket.

Draw a picture of your parents. Put this picture in your paper plate pocket.

Materials
paper plates
stapler
3" x 5" (7.62 x 12.7 cm) sheets of paper
half sheets of paper
pen
pencil
markers
crayons
scissors

p ppppppppppppppppppppppppppppppppppppppppppppppppppppppp p

GA14

Peter Piper

Read the poem "Peter Piper Picked a Peck of Pickled Peppers." On a sheet of paper write all of the words that begin with the letter **p**. Write each different word only once.

Materials

a copy of the poem
paper
pencils

P Is for Pen Pals

A pen pal is a friend that you make by writing a letter to him. Write a letter to a pen pal. Put the letter into an envelope and put your pen pal's address on it. Your teacher will mail it for you.

Materials

a pen pal
paper
pencils
envelope
stamp

P Is for Pad

A pad can be several sheets of paper held together in some way. Take five 3" x 5" (7.62 x 12.7 cm) sheets of paper and staple them together by putting two staples across the top. On the top sheet of your paper pad make a list of the foods people eat that begin with the letter **p**.

On another sheet make a list of animals that people can have as pets. Use more sheets for your list if needed.

Materials

five 3" x 5" (7.62 x 12.7 cm) sheets of paper
stapler
pencils

GA1420

"Q" Writing Activities

Q QQQQQQQQQQQQQQQQQQQQQQQQQQQQQQQQQQQQQQQQQQQQ Q

q **Quarterbacks** q

Q What do quarterbacks do all day? Q

q Fold a sheet of paper into four boxes. q

Q In each box draw a picture of a quarterback doing something. Q

q Write the name of the play at the bottom. q

Q Fill up the front of the sheet. Q

q Try to fill up the back of the sheet. q

Q Q

q **Materials** q

Q paper Q

q pencils q

Q crayons Q

q qqqqqqqqqqqqqqqqqqqqqqqqqqqqqqqqqqqqqqqqqqqqqqqqqqqqq q

Q QQQQQQQQQQQQQQQQQQQQQQQQQQQQQQQQQQQQQQQQQQQQ Q

q **Quiet** q

Q So many times we are asked to be quiet. Q

q Write some directions to children who don't know when to be quiet. q

Q Start each sentence like this: "Be quiet when _____." Q

q q

Q **Materials** Q

q 12" x 18" (30.48 x 45.72 cm) paper q

Q pencils Q

q qqqqqqqqqqqqqqqqqqqqqqqqqqqqqqqqqqqqqqqqqqqqqqqqqqqqq q

Be quiet when the teacher is talking.

Q QQQQQQQQQQQQQQQQQQQQQQQQQQQQQQQQQQQQQQQQQQQQ Q

q **Queen's Crown** q

Q Make a crown from the yellow paper. Q

q Write *Queen's Crown* on the crown. q

Q Decorate the crown with **q** words. Q

q q

Q **Materials** Q

q 6" x 18" (15.24 x 45.72 cm) yellow paper q

Q shiny jewel stickers Q

q crayons q

Q pencils Q

q qqqqqqqqqqqqqqqqqqqqqqqqqqqqqqqqqqqqqqqqqqqqqqqqqqqqq q

Queen's Crown

GA1

Q QQQQQQQQQQQQQQQQQQQQQQQQQQQQQQQQQQQQQQQ Q

Quick

What things are quick? Draw a large **Q** on a sheet of paper. Cut it out. Write Quick on your Q. Get with a friend. Work together to fill the Q's with quick things.

Materials
paper
scissors
pencils

qqqqqqqqqqqqqqqqqqqqqqqqqqqqqqqqqqqqqqqqqqqqqqqqqqqqqqqqqq

Q QQQQQQQQQQQQQQQQQQQQQQQQQQQQQQQQQQQQQQQ Q

Quartet of Quackers

Take four sheets of square paper. On each piece draw a duck. Cut out each duck. On each round sheet of paper, write *quack* as many times as you can get it on the sheet. Glue the quacks to the duck's mouth. Glue all quackers on a sheet of paper. Write *Quartet of Quackers* at the top.

Materials
Per child:
four squares of paper 6" x 6" (15.24 x 15.24 cm)
four circles 2" (5.08 cm) each
12" x 18" (30.48 x 45.72 cm) paper
crayons
scissors
pencils

qqqqqqqqqqqqqqqqqqqqqqqqqqqqqqqqqqqqqqqqqqqqqqqqqqqqqqqqqq

Q QQQQQQQQQQQQQQQQQQQQQQQQQQQQQQQQQQQQQQQ Q

Quotes

Quotes are something someone says.
Ask a friend to say something.
Write down exactly what he says.
At the top write "Quoted from _____."
Get many quotes from one friend or one quote from many friends.

Materials
paper
pencils

qqqqqqqqqqqqqqqqqqqqqqqqqqqqqqqqqqqqqqqqqqqqqqqqqqqqqqqqqq

GA1420

"R" Writing Activities

R RRRRRRRRRRRRRRRRRRRRRRRRRRRRRRRRRRRRRRRRRRRRRRRRRRRRRR R
r **R Is for Rules** r
R Make a list of the classroom rules your teacher wants you to obey. R
r Draw a line under the one rule that is the most difficult for you to obey. r
R Make a list of the rules your parents want you to obey. R
r Draw a circle around the one rule that is the most difficult for you to obey. r
R R
r r
R **Materials** R
r paper r
R pencils R
r rrrrrrrrrrrrrrrrrrrrrrrrrrrrrrrrrrrrrrrrrrrrrrrrrrrrrrrrrrrrrrrrrrrrrrrrrrrrr r

R RRRRRRRRRRRRRRRRRRRRRRRRRRRRRRRRRRRRRRRRRRRRRRRRRRRRRR R
r **R Is for River** r
R Make a list of the things you can do in, on, or next to a river. R
r Draw a picture of your favorite thing you have on your list. r
R R
r r
R **Materials** R
r paper r
R pencils R
r rrrrrrrrrrrrrrrrrrrrrrrrrrrrrrrrrrrrrrrrrrrrrrrrrrrrrrrrrrrrrrrrrrrrrrrrrrrrr r

R RRRRRRRRRRRRRRRRRRRRRRRRRRRRRRRRRRRRRRRRRRRRRRRRRRRRRR R
r **R Is for Read** r
R Make a list of your favorite books. R
r r
R R
r **Materials** r
R paper R
r pencils r
R rrrrrrrrrrrrrrrrrrrrrrrrrrrrrrrrrrrrrrrrrrrrrrrrrrrrrrrrrrrrrrrrrrrrrrrrrrrrr R

R RRRRRRRRRRRRRRRRRRRRRRRRRRRRRRRRRRRRRRRRRRRRRRRRRRRRRR R
r **R Is for Relax** r
R On a sheet of paper, tell how you or one of your family members likes R
r to relax. r
R rrrrrrrrrrrrrrrrrrrrrrrrrrrrrrrrrrrrrrrrrrrrrrrrrrrrrrrrrrrrrrrrrrrrrrrrrrrrr R

GA1420

R RRRRRRRRRRRRRRRRRRRRRRRRRRRRRRRRRRRRRRRRRRRRRRRRRRRRRRR R

R Is for Remainder

The remainder is what you call the answer to a subtraction problem. On a sheet of paper do ten subtraction problems and circle the remainder in each.

Materials
sheet of subtraction problems

⬭ 10

r rrrrrrrrrrrrrrrrrrrrrrrrrrrrrrrrrrrrrrrrrrrrrrrrrrrrrrrrrrrrrrrrrrrrrrrrrrrrrrrrrrrrrrrrrrrrr r

R RRRRRRRRRRRRRRRRRRRRRRRRRRRRRRRRRRRRRRRRRRRRRRRRRRRRRRR R

R Is for Round

Make a list of things that are round on a sheet of paper that is cut into a circle.

On a second sheet make a list of words that begin with the letter **r**.

On a third sheet make a list of things that can be recycled.

On a fourth sheet make a list of things that ring or you can make ring.

Put these sheets in order and staple them together at the top of the pages.

Materials
four sheets of paper cut into circles
pencils
stapler

run rake race / Cans bottles papers / bell phone

r rrrrrrrrrrrrrrrrrrrrrrrrrrrrrrrrrrrrrrrrrrrrrrrrrrrrrrrrrrrrrrrrrrrrrrrrrrrrrrrrrrrrrrrrrrrrr r

R RRRRRRRRRRRRRRRRRRRRRRRRRRRRRRRRRRRRRRRRRRRRRRRRRRRRRRR R

R Is for Recipe

A recipe has the directions for making something good to eat. Choose something that you like to make to eat. Write the directions for making it on a sheet of paper.
Trade recipes with a friend.

Crunchy Cookies

r rrrrrrrrrrrrrrrrrrrrrrrrrrrrrrrrrrrrrrrrrrrrrrrrrrrrrrrrrrrrrrrrrrrrrrrrrrrrrrrrrrrrrrrrrrrrr r

"S" Writing Activities

SSSSSSSSSSSSSSSSSSSSSSSSSSSSSSSSSSSSSSSSSSSSSSSSSSSSSS

Seasons

Find three friends to work with.

Each friend takes one piece of paper.

Choose a season for each person.

Write the season name at the top of your paper.

Fold your paper into four boxes.

Each friend tells one thing to do each season.

Write this in one of your boxes.

When all four boxes are full, draw pictures.

Materials

paper

crayons or markers

pencils

sssssssssssssssssssssssssssssssssssssssssssssssssssssssssssss

SSSSSSSSSSSSSSSSSSSSSSSSSSSSSSSSSSSSSSSSSSSSSSSSSSSSSS

Send Stories on Stationery

People who do not live close to you like to receive mail.

On a piece of stationery, write a story about you.

Draw pictures to illustrate the story.

Take your story home to send to someone.

Materials

stationery

pencils

crayons or markers

sssssssssssssssssssssssssssssssssssssssssssssssssssssssssssss

SSSSSSSSSSSSSSSSSSSSSSSSSSSSSSSSSSSSSSSSSSSSSSSSSSSSSS

Songs

Write the names of songs you know on the notes. Post near the piano or take them home.

Materials

giant musical notes

pencils or pens

sssssssssssssssssssssssssssssssssssssssssssssssssssssssssssss

Store

Take one large sheet of white paper.
Take three strips of brown paper.
Glue the strips onto the white sheet to make shelves.
Make products for your store out of construction paper.
Label each product.

Materials

12" x 18" (30.48 x 45.72 cm) white paper
1" x 18" (2.54 x 45.72 cm) brown strips
glue
construction paper scraps
scissors
pencils
crayons and markers

Seashore

Work with a friend.
Each pair needs two sheets of blue paper and one tan.
Cut the tan one in half using a jagged wavy line to cut on.
Each friend takes a tan one to glue onto a blue one. This makes the sea and the shore.
Make things from construction paper that belong in the sea or on the shore.
Label each.

Materials

blue paper
tan paper
scissors
glue
pencils
paper scraps

GA1420

"T" Writing Activities

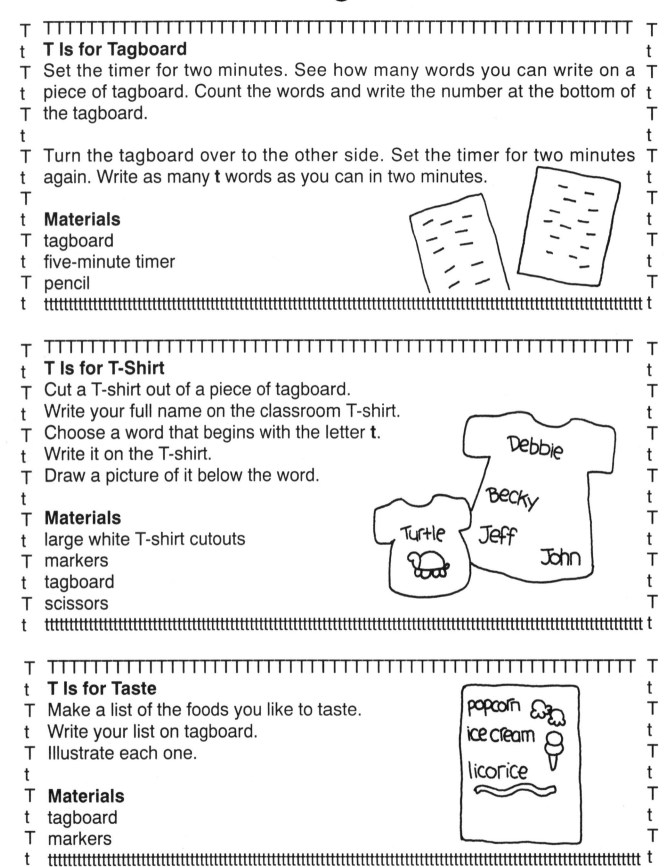

T Is for Tagboard

Set the timer for two minutes. See how many words you can write on a piece of tagboard. Count the words and write the number at the bottom of the tagboard.

Turn the tagboard over to the other side. Set the timer for two minutes again. Write as many **t** words as you can in two minutes.

Materials
tagboard
five-minute timer
pencil

T Is for T-Shirt
Cut a T-shirt out of a piece of tagboard.
Write your full name on the classroom T-shirt.
Choose a word that begins with the letter **t**.
Write it on the T-shirt.
Draw a picture of it below the word.

Materials
large white T-shirt cutouts
markers
tagboard
scissors

T Is for Taste
Make a list of the foods you like to taste.
Write your list on tagboard.
Illustrate each one.

Materials
tagboard
markers

GA14

T Is for Tablet

On a sheet of paper in your tablet, make a list of the television shows you like to watch. Draw a circle around your favorite show.

On a second sheet of paper in your tablet, make a list of your school subjects. Write the name of your best subject and tell why you like it.

On a third sheet of paper in your tablet, make a list of camping words such as *tent*.

Materials
tablet
pencil

T Is for Ticket

Make a list of things for which you need tickets.

On a 2" x 4" (5.08 x 10.16 cm) piece of tagboard, print the words needed for a movie ticket.

Materials
2" x 4" (5.08 x 10.16 cm) piece of tagboard
thin-line black marker
paper
pencil

T Is for Tissue

Make a list of things for which you can use tissues.

Take several tissues and make something. On a 3" x 5" (7.62 x 12.7 cm) index card tell about your creation.

Materials
tissues
3" x 5" (7.62 x 12.7 cm) index cards
markers
rubber bands
tape

GA1420

"U" Writing Activities

Umpires

Take one piece of paper.

Fold it in half. Open it up.

Draw an umpire on the left side of the paper.

On the right side write things an umpire says.

Try: You're out.

Materials

paper

pencils

crayons

Umbrella

Make an umbrella out of construction paper.

Glue it to a sheet of paper.

Draw a person under the umbrella.

Make a rainy scene.

Label all of the parts of your pictures.

Put a piece of Saran Wrap over your picture to make it shiny like water.

Materials

paper

pencils

crayons

Saran Wrap

Up

Sit where you are for a minute.

Look up.

What do you see when you look up?

Make a list of things you see when you look up.

Materials

paper

pencils

GA142

Underline

Find a partner to work with.
Each person takes a piece of paper.
Write ten **u** words and ten other words on the paper.
Give your paper to your partner.
Underline all of the **u** words.
Copy all of the **u** words onto a giant **U**.

Materials

paper
pencils
one giant **U** cut from a 12" x 9" (30.48 x 22.86 cm) sheet of paper per child

Unsafe

Take a circle.
Color the outside edge of the circle red.
List things that are unsafe to do on the circle.
Glue a red strip across the circle.

Materials

9" (22.86 cm) white circle
9" x 1" (22.86 x 2.54 cm) red strip of paper
pencils

Utensils

Many utensils are used in a kitchen.
Take one sheet of white paper, one strip of brown paper. Write *Utensils* on the brown strip.
Glue the brown strip across the top of your white sheet.
Draw kitchen utensils (like a spatula) hanging from the brown strip.
Label each utensil.

Materials

12" x 18" (30.48 x 45.72 cm) white paper
1" x 18" (2.54 x 45.72 cm) brown strip
crayons
pencils

GA1420

"V" Writing Activities

V Is for Vegetables

At the top of a sheet of paper write the word *Vegetables*. Divide the rest of the sheet of paper into two rows. At the top of the row to the left print "Those I Like," and at the top of the row to the right print "Those I Don't Like." Write the names of vegetables that you like in the left row and the names of vegetables you don't like in the row to the right.

Print the names of vegetables on 3" x 5" (7.62 x 12.7 cm) sheets of paper, one name to a sheet. Use a color of marker or crayon that matches the color of the vegetable.

Draw and color pictures of vegetables. Cut out the pictures and glue them on a sheet of construction paper. Write the word *Vegetables* at the top of the paper.

Materials
3" x 5" (7.62 x 12.7 cm) sheets of paper
markers or crayons
scissors
construction paper

V Is for Valentines

Draw and color valentines for several of your classmates. Try to do very well.

Materials
drawing paper
pencils
crayons
markers
scissors

V Is for Vast

Vast means "very large or big." Make a list of other words that mean large or big. Print the words with large letters and use fat crayons or markers.

Materials
fat crayons
markers

V Is for Vote

Cut out ads from the newspaper for people who are running for public office. Make a list of the people you would vote for if you could vote.

Materials
newspapers
scissors
paper
pencils

V Is for Vacation

Families often go on vacations during the summer or on holidays. On a sheet of paper tell about a vacation you and your family took.

V Is for Vehicles

Vehicle is another word for a machine in which you can ride. Make a list of the things you can ride in.

One type of vehicle is a car or automobile. Make a list of kinds of cars. Draw a circle around the kind of car or cars your family owns.

Materials
books about vehicles

GA1420

"W" Writing Activities

W WWWWWWWWWWWWWWWWWWWWWWWWWWWWWWWWWWWWWWWWWWWWW W

w **Wallet**

W Make a wallet out of a piece of brown construction paper.

w Fold the paper up once and tape the edges.

W Make some things to carry in your wallet.

w Write the right words on them.

W Put them in your wallet.

w

W **Materials**

w 6" x 9" (15.24 x 22.86 cm) brown paper

W construction paper scraps

w pencils

W crayons

w tape

w wwwwwwwwwwwwwwwwwwwwwwwwwwwwwwwwwwwwwwwwwwwww w

W WWWWWWWWWWWWWWWWWWWWWWWWWWWWWWWWWWWWWWWWWWWW W

w **Water**

W Water is in many places.

w Fold a piece of paper into eight boxes.

W Draw a different place for water in each box.

w Label each picture.

W Try tub or lake.

w

W **Materials**

w paper

W crayons

w pencils

w wwwwwwwwwwwwwwwwwwwwwwwwwwwwwwwwwwwwwwwwwwwww w

W WWWWWWWWWWWWWWWWWWWWWWWWWWWWWWWWWWWWWWWWWWWW W

w **What's Wooden?**

W Get a scrap of wood and a pencil.

w Walk around your room.

W Look for things that are made of wood.

w Write the names of things made of wood on your scrap of wood.

w

W **Materials**

w scraps of wood

W pencils

w wwwwwwwwwwwwwwwwwwwwwwwwwwwwwwwwwwwwwwwwwwwww w

GA142

Wastebasket

Cover a can to make it look like a wastebasket.
Write **w** words on strips of paper.
Place the **w** words in the wastebasket.
Switch with a friend.
Read each other's **w** words.

Materials

one juice can per child
1" (2.54 cm) strips of paper the height of the can
construction paper
pencils
glue

Watch

Usually a watch has numbers on it.
Make a watch that has number words on it.

Materials

one 12" (30.48 cm) circle per child
1" x 4" (2.54 x 10.16 cm) strips of black construction paper
1" x 3" (2.54 x 7.62 cm) strips of black construction paper
pencils

Web or W Words

Take a sheet of black paper.
Make a path of Elmer's glue from corner to corner.
Glue on white yarn.
Do the same from the other two corners.
Starting in the center make circles of glue.
Place yarn on each circle.
Write **w** words on strips of paper.
Glue them into the web.

Materials

black paper
glue
white strips of yarn
1" x 3" (2.54 x 7.62 cm) white strips of paper

GA1420

"X," "Y" and "Z" Writing Activities

X XXXXXXXXXXXXXXXXXXXXXXXXXXXXXXXXXXXXXXXXXXXXXXXXXXX X

X Is for X ray

An X ray allows doctors to see or look through the covering of the body. Look through Pictionary or a dictionary and make a list of words that have the letter **x** in them.

Materials

Pictionary
dictionary
paper
pencils

x xxxxxxxxxxxxxxxxxxxxxxxxxxxxxxxxxxxxxxxxxxxxxxxxxxxx x

X XXXXXXXXXXXXXXXXXXXXXXXXXXXXXXXXXXXXXXXXXXXXXXXX X

X Is for Tic-Tac-Toe

The game tic-tac-toe is played with X's and O's. With a classmate play eleven games of tic-tac-toe.

Materials

paper
pencils

x xxxxxxxxxxxxxxxxxxxxxxxxxxxxxxxxxxxxxxxxxxxxxxxxxxxxxx x

Y YYYYYYYYYYYYYYYYYYYYYYYYYYYYYYYYYYYYYYYYYYYYYYYYYYYY Y

Y Is for Yesterday

Make a list of things you did yesterday. Circle those things that were hard. Draw a line under those that were easy.

y yyyyyyyyyyyyyyyyyyyyyyyyyyyyyyyyyyyyyyyyyyyyyyyyyyyyyyyy y

Y YYYYYYYYYYYYYYYYYYYYYYYYYYYYYYYYYYYYYYYYYYYYYYYYYYYY Y

Y Is for Yard

On a sheet of construction paper draw and color a picture of your back or front yard. Add all of the things you have or would like to have in your yard. Write the name of each item beside it in your picture.

Materials

construction paper
crayons
markers
pencils

y yyyyyyyyyyyyyyyyyyyyyyyyyyyyyyyyyyyyyyyyyyyyyyyyyyyyyyyyyyyy Y

132

Y Is for Yellow

Make a list of things that are yellow.

Y Is for You

Make a list of words that begin with **y**. Use Pictionary or a dictionary to help you think of **y** words.

Materials

Pictionary
dictionary
paper
pencils

Z Is for Zoo

Make a list of the animals that you have seen in a zoo.

Draw, color and cut out pictures of three animals that you have seen in a zoo. Now draw, color and cut out three cages large enough to put over each animal. Glue the animals on a sheet of construction paper. Then glue the cages over the animals, so that the animals can be seen through the cages. Draw, color and cut out a small sign with each animal's name on it. Glue each sign on the animal's cage. Finally, make a sign for the top of the page with the word *Zoo* on it.

Materials

drawing paper
construction paper
scissors
crayons or markers
glue
pencils

Z Is for Zipper

Zippers hold things closed or together. Make a list of other words that hold things closed or together.

GA1420

"Wh" Writing Activities

WhWhWhWhWhWhWhWhWhWhWhWhWhWhWhWhWhWhWhWh

What, When and Where

Think about what you do each day.

Take one sheet of paper.

Fold it into three boxes.

Write *What* in the first column at the top.

Write *When* in the middle at the top.

Write *Where* in the last column at the top.

In the first column make a list of things you do all day.

In the next column write when you do them.

In the last column write where you do them.

Materials

12" x 18" (30.48 x 45.72 cm) paper

pencils

markers

whwhwhwhwhwhwhwhwhwhwhwhwhwhwhwhwhwhwhwh

WhWhWhWhWhWhWhWhWhWhWhWhWhWhWhWhWhWhWhWh

What, When and Where

Choose your favorite thing to do all day.

Take one sheet of paper.

Fold it into thirds.

Write *What* in the first column at the top.

Write *When* in the middle at the top.

Write *Where* in the last column at the top.

In the left part of the paper draw a picture of your favorite thing to do.

In the middle column write when you do it.

On the right side of the paper draw the room where you do it.

Materials

paper

pencils

crayons or markers

whwhwhwhwhwhwhwhwhwhwhwhwhwhwhwhwhwhwhwh

GA142

Wh WhWhWhWhWhWhWhWhWhWhWhWhWhWhWhWhWhWhWhWhWh   Wh

Whales Are Whoppers

Whales are huge mammals.

Make a list of all the words that mean "huge."

Now tell about having the whale live in your house.

Use your "huge" words in the story.

The whale would need a gigantic bed, etc.

Draw a picture to go with your story.

Materials

paper

crayons

pencils

whwhwhwhwhwhwhwhwhwhwhwhwhwhwhwhwhwhwhwhwhwhwh

Wh WhWhWhWhWhWhWhWhWhWhWhWhWhWhWhWhWhWhWhWhWh   Wh

What's White?

Many things in your room are white.

Choose a piece of colored paper.

Draw or paint pictures of white things on the paper.

Make some pictures on white construction paper.

Use some cotton balls on your picture.

Write about your pictures with white crayon.

Materials

white construction paper	white crayons
colored construction paper	white chalks
scissors	white tempera
glue	brushes

whwhwhwhwhwhwhwhwhwhwhwhwhwhwhwhwhwhwhwhwhwhwh

Wh WhWhWhWhWhWhWhWhWhWhWhWhWhWhWhWhWhWhWhWhWh   Wh

Are Whirlybirds Birds?

Find a friend.

Make a list of all the birds you know that are not birds.

Materials

paper

pencils

whwhwhwhwhwhwhwhwhwhwhwhwhwhwhwhwhwhwhwhwhwhwh

GA1420

"Sh" Writing Activities

Sh ShShShShShShShShShShShShShShShShShShShShShShShSh Sh
Sh **Shipwrecked** Sh
Sh Your ship wrecks and you are stranded on an island. Sh
Sh Take one sheet of storywriting paper. Sh
Sh At the top, draw a picture showing how you will live on the island. Sh
Sh At the bottom of the paper on the lines, write about being shipwrecked. Sh
Sh Sh
Sh **Materials** Sh
Sh storywriting paper Sh
Sh pencils Sh
Sh crayons Sh
Sh markers Sh
Sh shshshshshshshshshshshshshshshshshshshshshshshshshsh Sh

Sh ShShShShShShShShShShShShShShShShShShShShShShShSh Sh
Sh **Shoes** Sh
Sh Get a large sheet of paper. Sh
Sh Find a friend. Sh
Sh Trace his shoes onto your paper. Sh
Sh Color them the right colors. Sh
Sh Write the name of your friend next to the shoes. Sh
Sh Fill your paper with many friends' shoes. Sh
Sh Sh
Sh **Materials** Sh
Sh butcher paper Sh
Sh crayons Sh
Sh pencils Sh
Sh shshshshshshshshshshshshshshshshshshshshshshshshshsh

Sh ShShShShShShShShShShShShShShShShShShShShShShShSh Sh
Sh **Shirts with Autographs** Sh
Sh Place a cardboard shirt inside a T-shirt. Sh
Sh Ask a friend to autograph your T-shirt. Sh
Sh Fill your shirt with the names of all your classmates. Sh
Sh Sh
Sh **Materials** Sh
Sh T-shirts Sh
Sh fabric paints or markers Sh
Sh cardboard shirts Sh
Sh shshshshshshshshshshshshshshshshshshshshshshshshshsh Sh

GA1

Sh

Shortcake

How do you make shortcake?
Take a "recipe" card.
Write a recipe for shortcake on the recipe card.
Illustrate the steps.
Talk your teacher into making real shortcake.

Materials

5" x 8" (12.7 x 20.32 cm) index cards
pencils
crayons
shshshshshshshshshshshshshshshshshshshshshshsh

ShShShShShShShShShShShShShShShShShShShShShShShSh

Shabby and Sharp Shapes

Make a list of all the shapes you know on a sheet of paper.
Tear each shape out of paper.
Glue it on one sheet of paper.
Write *Shabby Shapes* on it.
Cut each shape out of paper.
Glue it on a different sheet of paper.
Write *Sharp Shapes* on it.
Write the name of each shape on or below it.

Materials

scissors
construction paper
scraps
glue
pencils
shshshshshshshshshshshshshshshshshshshshshshshshs

ShShShShShShShShShShShShShShShShShShShShShShShSh

Shelf Shopping

Make a shelf on a piece of paper. Out of construction paper make things to put on the shelves. Swap with a freind. Write a shopping list for each shelf.

Materials

construction paper
scissors
glue
paper
pencils
shshshshshshshshshshshshshshshshshshshshshshshshshs

"Ch" Writing Activities

Ch ChChChChChChChChChChChChChChChChChChChChChChChCh Ch
Ch **Chest** Ch
Ch Take one sheet of construction paper and round off the top two corners. Ch
Ch Decorate it with gold or silver. Staple a sheet of white paper to the back. Ch
Ch Write all the words you know from the dictionary that begin with **ch**. Ch
Ch Ch
Ch **Materials** Ch
Ch construction paper Ch
Ch pencils Ch
Ch white paper Ch
Ch gold and silver scraps or stickers Ch
Ch scissors Ch
Ch stapler Ch
Ch chchchchchchchchchchchchchchchchchchchchchchchchch Ch

Ch ChChChChChChChChChChChChChChChChChChChChChChChChCh Ch
Ch **Chunky** Ch
Ch Make a list of all the foods that are chunky. Draw a picture of three of the Ch
Ch foods. Illustrate them to show that they are chunky. Ch
Ch Ch
Ch **Materials** Ch
Ch paper Ch
Ch pencils Ch
Ch scissors Ch
Ch scraps Ch
Ch glue Ch
Ch crayons Ch
Ch chchchchchchchchchchchchchchchchchchchchchchchchch Ch

Ch ChChChChChChChChChChChChChChChChChChChChChChChChCh Ch
Ch **Chopper** Ch
Ch Write directions on how to chop up a banana. Put a piece of waxed paper Ch
Ch on your table first. Chop a banana. Find a friend and read his directions. Ch
Ch Try to do it the way his directions say. Ch
Ch Ch
Ch **Materials** Ch
Ch paper Ch
Ch pencils Ch
Ch bananas Ch
Ch table knives Ch
Ch waxed paper Ch
Ch chchchchchchchchchchchchchchchchchchchchchchchchchch Ch

Ch ChChChChChChChChChChChChChChChChChChChChChChCh Ch
Ch Choosing Chicken
Ch Draw a picture of a unique chicken or make a chicken from the materials
Ch available. Describe your chicken in an ad. Place your chicken on the
Ch bulletin board with all the other chickens. The teacher will read your ad
Ch and have your friends choose your chicken.
Ch
Ch **Materials**
Ch paper
Ch pencils
Ch feathers
Ch glue
Ch scissors
Ch scraps
Ch chchchchchchchchchchchchchchchchchchchchchchchchchch Ch

Ch ChChChChChChChChChChChChChChChChChChChChChChCh Ch
Ch Chilly
Ch What makes you chilly? Number a sheet of paper on every third line. On
Ch each line write "I get chilly when _____." Finish each sentence in a
Ch different way. Try this one for a starter: I get chilly when I get out of the
Ch swimming pool.
Ch
Ch **Materials**
Ch wide-lined paper
Ch pencils
Ch chchchchchchchchchchchchchchchchchchchchchchchchchch Ch

Ch ChChChChChChChChChChChChChChChChChChChChChChCh Ch
Ch Checkers
Ch Find a partner to play checkers with. Take a piece of paper and pencil with
Ch you. Each time one of you makes a move, write about it. When you are
Ch finished, try to read your directions and play the same game again.
Ch
Ch **Materials**
Ch checkers game
Ch paper
Ch pencils
Ch chchchchchchchchchchchchchchchchchchchchchchchchchch Ch

"Th" Writing Activities

Th ThThThThThThThThThThThThThThThThThThThThThThThThThThThTh Th

Th **Thermometer**

Th When the weather is cold the thermometer is low.

Th When it is hot, the thermometer is high.

Th Fold your paper in half lengthwise. On one side put numbers down the left

Th and color in a red line for a high temperature in the summer. On the other

Th side, put numbers on the right and color in a red line for a low temperature

Th in the winter.

Th **Materials**

Th paper

Th pencils

Th red crayon

Th thththththththththththththththththththththththththththththththththththth

Th ThThThThThThThThThThThThThThThThThThThThThThThThThThThTh Th

Th **Th Is for Thankful**

Th Write a thank-you note to someone for doing something nice for you.

Th Illustrate the note and make it colorful.

Th

Th **Materials**

Th paper

Th pencils

Th markers or crayons

Th thththththththththththththththththththththththththththththththththththth

Th ThThThThThThThThThThThThThThThThThThThThThThThThThThThTh Th

Th **Throne**

Th Kings and queens sit on thrones. Draw a picture of a king or queen sitting

Th on a throne. Write the word *throne* beside the picture. Wouldn't it be a

Th thrill to sit on a throne? Draw a picture of you sitting on a throne next to

Th the king or queen.

Th **Materials**

Th paper

Th crayons or markers

Th thththththththththththththththththththththththththththththththththththth

GA

Th ThThThThThThThThThThThThThThThThThThThThThThThThThThThThThTh Th

Th Is for Three

Make a list of the number words that begin with the letters **th**. Write each word three times.

Materials
paper
pencils

thththththththththththththththththththththththththththththththththththth

thirty - thirty - thirty

Th ThThThThThThThThThThThThThThThThThThThThThThThThThThThThTh Th

Th Is for Think

Think about words. Look around the classroom.
Make a list of words that name things in your classroom.
Circle all of the words that contain the letters **th** together.

Materials
paper
pencils

thththththththththththththththththththththththththththththththththththth

Math book

Th ThThThThThThThThThThThThThThThThThThThThThThThThThThThTh Th

Th Is for Thirsty

When you are thirsty, what do you like to drink to take away your thirst?
First, make a list of drinks you could have to take away your thirst. Then cut out pictures of things to drink from magazines.
Glue these pictures on a sheet of paper. Write the name of each drink beside it.

Materials
paper   scissors
pencils   glue
magazines

thththththththththththththththththththththththththththththththththththth

milk   pop
orange juice

Th ThThThThThThThThThThThThThThThThThThThThThThThThThThThTh Th

Thorn

Some plants like rosebushes have thorns. These thorns help protect the plant. Draw a picture of a rosebush. Include thorns on the bush. Now label all of the thorns.

Materials
paper
pencils
crayons

thththththththththththththththththththththththththththththththththththth

GA1420

Writing Center

Center Placement

Put the writing center in a quiet area of the room where children will not easily be distracted. The lighting should be good and the atmosphere pleasant.

Center Equipment

The center should contain shelves for storing of materials and supplies, small tables for children to write on, chairs sized to fit the tables and the children, and a bulletin board nearby for posting writing activities (see pages 86-141).

Center Materials

The center should contain a variety of materials. Try these for starters.

alphabet charts	dictionaries	Pictionaries
stationery	envelopes	story paper
lined paper, various sizes/shapes	unlined paper, various sizes/shapes	note pads
notebooks	journals	Post-its
3" x 5" (7.62 x 12.7 cm) index cards	5" x 8" (12.7 x 20.32 cm) index cards	scissors
		markers
glue	pencils	pens
erasers	Liquid Paper	

Objectives Met at a Writing Center

Language: Children learn to write what they are thinking and to read what they write.

Children talk while they write.

Children write meaningful messages to others and get responses.

Children practice word building skills, sentence formation and punctuation.

Math: Children make lists of things that they need, count them and record the numbers.

Social Studies: Children write letters or notes to others and receive responses.

Children can get pen pals from other parts of the country.

Children learn to write thank-you's and invitations.

Motor Skills: Children practice using fine motor skills with meaningful print.

Art: Children can illustrate their writings.

Information modified from *Centers for Early Learners Throughout the Year*, Jeri A. Carroll, Good Apple, 1991.

GA142

All About Me

This Is How I Feel
Take one paper plate.
Write your name on the back of it.
Make a list of all the different feelings you have on the back of the plate.
On the front of the plate decorate a face like one of the feelings.

Materials
paper plates
glue
pencils
yarn
googlie eyes
crayons
scraps of paper

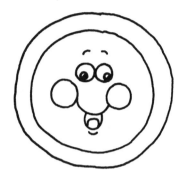

All Dressed Up and Ready to Go
Draw a picture of yourself in your favorite outfit.
Label each piece of clothing.

Materials
paper
pencils
crayons

Footwork
Get a piece of paper and a pencil.
Take off your shoe.
Trace around your foot.
Write a list of all the things your foot can do on your traced foot.

Materials
paper
pencils
scissors

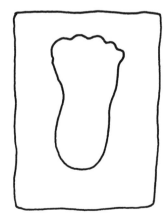

Handiwork
(Try the above activity with your hand.)

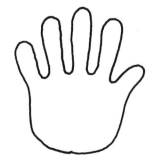

GA1420

Me and My Friends

Together We Stand
With a partner trace around your body on a
piece of brown butcher paper. Cut it out.
Write about all the things you like to do
with your friend on your traced body.
Decorate the body.
Post the pictures in the hallway, holding
hands with your partner.

Materials
butcher paper
crayons
scissors
scrap box
pencils
markers
yarn

Do You Want to Play?
Get one piece of paper. Fold it into eight boxes.
Draw a toy in each box.
Cut up the boxes so you have eight rectangles, each with a toy on it.
Find a friend.
Play Concentration.
Do you have any matches?

Materials
paper
crayons
scissors

In the Pool
Get a piece of blue construction paper.
Plan a party for a few favorite friends.
Make a list of friends to invite.
Make a list of games to play in the water at your party.

Materials
blue construction paper
crayons
pencils

At School

What's on the Playground?
Draw a picture of your school's playground.
Label all the things in your picture.
Go outside.
Put glue on the bottom edge of your paper.
Place the glued side in the sand.

Materials
paper
crayons
scissors
glue and sand

What's in Your Schoolroom?
Get a red piece of paper.
Sit on the floor. Look all around you.
Draw a small picture of things you see.
Go back to a table or your desk.
Write the word next to each picture.

Materials
red paper
pencils
crayons

What Do We Do All Day?
Make a list of all the things that you do all day.
Cut out each of these words or sentences.
What do you do in the morning? Put it first.
Put all the things you do all day in order from first to last.
Have a friend check the order.
Glue them onto a piece of paper in the right order.

Materials
pencils
crayons
glue
construction paper
paper

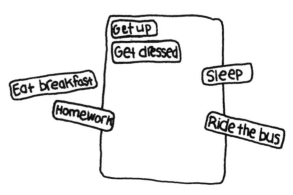

GA1420

Our Town

Where Do You Live?
Stuff a brown lunch sack with newspaper.
Fold over the top and staple it.
Get a piece of 6" x 6" (15.24 x 15.24 cm) construction paper.
Fold it in half.
Write your address on the paper.
Put it on top of your sack for a roof.
Find more roofs.
Have friends write their addresses on the roofs.
Keep them all together as an address book.
Put them on the top of your house to see what they look like.

Materials
paper sack
newspaper
staples
6" x 6" (15.24 x 15.24 cm) construction paper

Community Helpers
Get a box and some white paper.
Trace around the box sides onto the white paper.
Cut out the pieces.
Draw a picture of a helper on each piece.
Glue them to the sides of the box.
List what each community helper does on a piece of white paper. Put the lists in the box.
Find a friend.
Read the list to the friend and have him find the right helper.

Materials
box
paper
pencils
scissors
crayons
markers

GA1420

My State

Where in the State Have You Been?

Draw an outline of your state.
Cut it out.
List all the places you've been in your state.
Read them to a friend.
See if he has any places you have forgotten.
Add them to your list.

Materials
state shapes
paper
pencils

Who Do You Know in Your State?

Draw an outline of your state.
Cut it out.
List all the relatives, friends and other important people you know who live in your state.

Materials
state shapes
paper
pencils

Animals in My State

Draw an outline of your state.
Cut it out.
On small squares of paper draw pictures of the different animals that live in your state.
Glue them to the state shape.
Label each of the animals.

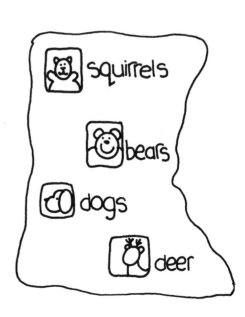

Materials
pencils
crayons
state shapes
paper
scissors
glue
3" x 3" (7.62 x 7.62 cm) squares of white paper

The Good Ol' USA

Picking Up the Pieces

Get a map puzzle of the United States.
Take out all of the pieces.
Find one state to put in the puzzle.
Write the name of the state on a sheet of paper before you put it in the puzzle.
When you have finished, dump the pieces out.
Put the puzzle together in the same order you did it last time.

Materials

United States puzzle
paper
pencils

What's in a State?

Pick a state you know about.
Write the name of that state at the top of a piece of paper.
Make a list of things you know about that state.
Make a list of people you know in the state.

Materials

United States map
paper
pencils

States in Order

Write the alphabet letters down the left side of a piece of paper.
Next to each letter write the names of states that start with that letter.
How many states did you name?
Which letter had the most?
Which letter had none?

Materials

paper
pencils

The Color of My World

What's Orange?

Get a sheet of orange construction paper.
Cut the paper into the shape of an orange.
Write the names of all the things that are orange.
Draw a picture of your favorite orange thing.

Materials

orange construction paper
pencils
crayons
scissors

Bright and Yellow

Get a sheet of yellow construction paper.
Cut out a round shape for a sun.
Make a list of things you can do in the sun.
On the back draw a picture of your favorite thing to do in the sun.

Materials

yellow construction paper
crayons
pencils
scissors

Jump in the Sandbox

Get a sheet of tan construction paper.
Make a list of all the things you can do with sand.
Mark off a 1" (2.54 cm) border all around the paper.
Take your paper to the sandbox or sand table.
Fill the border of your paper with glue.
Place the glued side in the sand.

Materials

tan construction paper
pencils
glue
ruler
sand

GA1420

Shapes

What's a Square?
Cut out a square.
Make a list on the front of the square of all the things you know that are squares.
Pretend this square is something special.
Write about this special square on the back.

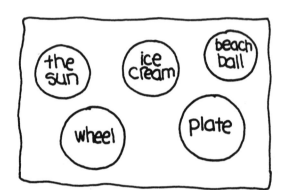

Materials
a square of paper
pencils

Round Up Some Circles
Cut out some circles.
Glue them to a piece of paper.
Think of what each might be.
Write one thing on each circle.

Materials
3" (7.62 cm) circles
9" x 12" (22.86 x 30.48 cm) construction paper
glue
pencils

All in a Diamond
A diamond can be a baseball diamond.
Cut out one diamond shape.
Make it look like a baseball diamond.
Label each part.
On the back make a list of all the baseball players you know.

Materials
a diamond shape
pencils
crayons

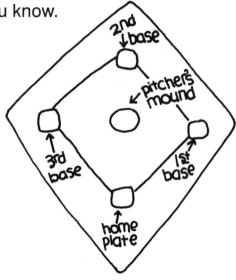

GA1420

Sizes

People Come in All Sizes

Get one sheet of large paper.
Fold it into three parts.
At the top of the first part write *Small*.
At the top of the second part write *Medium*.
At the top of the third write *Large*.
Draw a picture of you in the medium box.
Write names of people who are smaller than you in the small box.
Write names of people who are larger than you in the large box.
Write names of people your same size in the medium box.

Materials

paper
pencils
crayons

Light and Heavy

Sit near a set of scales.
Weigh two things.
Which one is lighter? Which one is heavier?
Write a sentence to tell which one is lighter.
Write a sentence to tell which one is heavier.
Here is an example:
  A feather is lighter than a rock.
  A rock is heavier than a feather.
Try lots of different things.

Materials

balance scale
pencils
paper

GA1420

Fun with Numbers

You Can Count on Me!

Think about numbers.

Get one sheet of paper.

List all the things about yourself that can be described by numbers (age is one).

Number your list.

Share your list with a friend.

Add the things you forgot to your list.

How many things are on your list?

Materials

paper

pencils

One, Two, Three, Four. . . .

Look around your classroom at all the things that can be counted.

Get a sheet of paper.

Write the numbers from one to twelve down the left side of the paper.

On the first line of your paper beside number one, write the name of something in your classroom that there is only one of.

Beside number two, write the name of something in your classroom that there are only two of.

Do the same with all the numbers up to twelve.

Show your list to a friend.

Circle all the words on your paper that are different than the ones on your friend's paper.

Materials

paper

pencils

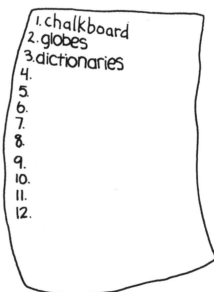

GA142

Bugs

Spiders

Draw a spider with eight legs.
Label the body parts.

Materials

spider picture
crayons
pencils

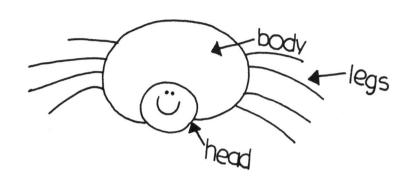

Ladybugs

Read the poem "Ladybug, Ladybug, Fly Away Home."
Get one sheet of paper and fold it in half.
At the top of one half write *Mom Ladybug*.
Under that write words that describe how the ladybug felt when she found out her house was on fire.
Draw a picture at the bottom.
At the top of the other half write *Children Ladybugs*.
Under that write words that describe how the children felt.
Draw a picture at the bottom.

Materials

paper
pencils
crayons

Bugs Buggin' Me

Draw a picture of you on a sheet of paper.
Draw bugs all over your paper, making sure you know what type each bug is.
Write the name of each bug beside it.

Materials

paper
pencils
crayons

GA1420

Writing Cats and Dogs

Would You Like to Ride?
Get a sheet of gray construction paper.
Draw an outline of an elephant and cut it out.
Write the names of all the animals that people can ride on the elephant shape.
Show your list to a friend and add the different animals on your friend's list to yours.

Materials
gray construction paper
pencils
scissors

The Circus Train
Take a sheet of 9" x 12" (22.86 x 30.48 cm) construction paper and fold it in half so that it is 9" x 6" (22.86 x 15.24 cm).
On each side draw a picture of a different animal.
Write the name of each animal you drew on a self-sticking label and paste it on the construction paper by its picture.
Stand your paper up on the counter or table and attach it to one of your class-mates' papers with string and tape.

Materials
construction paper
crayons
self-sticking labels
string
tape

GA142

Come and Get It!

Fruit Bowl
Make a list of all the names of fruit that you like to eat.
Draw and cut out a bowl of brown construction paper.
Draw and cut out all the kinds of fruit on your list.
Use construction paper that matches the color of the fruit you are including in your bowl.
Arrange the fruit on the paper bowl and glue it down.

Materials
construction paper of various colors
paper
scissors
pencils
crayons
markers
glue

Supper!
What is your favorite meal for supper?
On a sheet of paper make a list of all the foods that go with that meal.
Draw and cut out of construction paper pictures of the foods that go with your favorite meal.
Write the name of each food on its picture and glue it to a paper plate.
Suppertime!

Materials
paper
pencils
construction paper
crayons
markers
paper plates
glue

GA1420

Clothes

What Do I Wear All Day?
Get a large piece of paper.
Fold it into four boxes.
Number the boxes in order one to four.
In the first box draw a picture of you doing something first thing in the morning.
In the second box draw a picture of you doing something at noon.
In the third box draw a picture of you doing something in the afternoon.
In the last box draw a picture of you doing something in the evening.
Go back to each box and list the clothes that you have on in each picture.

Materials
paper
pencils
crayons

Can You Match Them Up?
Get scraps from the scrap box.
On each scrap draw a piece of clothing.
Cut it out.
Label it.
When you have several pieces of clothing, glue them onto a sheet of paper to make an outfit.
Draw a person's head and hands onto the clothing.

Materials
scraps
pencils
scissors
glue
crayons

GA142

No Place Like Home

What's in a Room?

Get a sheet of construction paper that is a similar color as the walls in your bedroom.

Make a list of the things that you have in your bedroom on the sheet of construction paper.

Turn the paper over and draw on it as many of the things from your list as you can.

Write your name across the top middle of your drawing.

Materials

construction paper
crayons

Setting the Table!

Get a piece of construction paper.

Use it as your place mat.

Across the top of the paper write your name.

Glue a paper plate, a paper cup, plastic silverware, and a napkin on your place mat.

Write the name of each thing you glued on your place mat beside it.

Decorate the rest of the area.

Materials

construction paper
paper plate
paper cup
plastic silverware
glue
crayons
napkin

     GA1420

On the Go

Cars Going By

Take a sheet of paper and crayons out onto the playground.

When a car goes by, make a mark on your paper with a crayon that is the color of the car going by.

When you get back inside, write about how many cars of each color you saw.

Here is an example: I saw _____ red cars.

Materials

paper
crayons
pencils

What Do Vehicles Do All Day?

Get a 12" x 18" (30.48 x 45.72 cm) sheet of paper. Fold it into eight boxes.

In each box draw a picture of a different type of vehicle.

Write its name at the top of the box.

At the bottom of the box write what it does.

Here is an example: A bus takes children to school.

Materials

paper
pencils
crayons

Children on the Go

List all the things that take you places.

Materials

paper
pencils

GA142